JOHN C. McLOUGHLIN · A New Look at

ARCHO

the Old Dinosaur   ALLEN LANE

SAURIA

ALLEN LANE
Penguin Books Ltd
17 Grosvenor Gardens
London SW1 OBD

First published in the United States of America by
The Viking Press 1979
First published in Great Britain by Allen Lane 1979
Copyright © John C. McLoughlin, 1979

ISBN 0 7139 1272 3

Set in Linotype Granjon
Printed in the United States of America

CONTENTS

This book is dedicated to
my grandmother, Ruth Merrill Barnett,
who has encouraged my education
in the natural sciences since
I was barely bipedal.

PREFACE

The study of paleontology, dealing as it does with creatures and events of the distant past, is necessarily rife with speculation. Our appreciation of such long-gone animals as dinosaurs is based on a few bits of mineralized bone and other meager clues, from which we must extrapolate across millions of years an entire era of spectacular evolutionary achievements. It is hardly odd, then, that the interpretations of identical material by two paleontologists may differ widely, colored as each is by individual prejudice and scientific orthodoxy.

The present work is a look at some of the modern interpretations of the life of the Mesozoic Era. Although the British naturalist Richard Owen suggested as early as 1841 that dinosaurs were metabolically advanced in the manner of mammals and birds, the prevailing view for more than a century and a half has relegated these highly successful animals to the status of reptiles. Now Owen's proposal is undergoing a new examination in the light of more advanced paleontologic technique, and a number of scientists are championing a radical reclassification of the higher vertebrates based on the results of this examination. Indeed, the Owen suggestion fills so many gaps and answers so many previously unanswered questions that we must include it in any consideration of dinosaur biology.

Most of the Grand Old Men of paleontology continue to support the point of view that dinosaurs were reptiles limited in activity by the temperatures of their environments. This conservatism is understandable in view of the fact that acceptance of the new theories would necessitate a major retooling of the world's museums to accommodate the new data—a remounting of skeletal restorations, for instance, that would cost millions of dollars. In addition, many of these Grand Old Men have spent lifetimes examining the Archosauria in conformance with the reptile orthodoxy, covering reams of paper with closely spaced print in support of same. Their acceptance of the new evidence might amount, in their eyes, to a surrender of years of work to the scientific wastebasket.

A few Young Turks, such as Robert T. Bakker of Johns Hopkins University, take a quite different point of view—that the immense success of the dinosaurs was based specifically on control of body temperature independent of environmental conditions. Other workers, such as Yale's John H. Ostrom, take positions between these extremes, suggesting, for example, that the carnivorous theropod dinosaurs were "warm-blooded" while the great herbivorous sauropods were not.

So it goes with any new theory in the scientific world—there are proponents and opponents. It will quickly become apparent that the author of this book is a proponent of advanced dinosaur metabolism, and that he has spent some time amassing data to support his point of view. In addition, the restorations appearing here are carefully liberal interpretations of the available data, rather strongly (I hope) suggestive of the dinosaurs' presumed metabolic sophistication. For instance, where econiches of extinct dinosaur and living mammal converge closely, I have provided the restored dinosaurs with color patterns approximating those of their modern counterparts. This liberty is taken in view of the fact that animals occupying similar niches usually converge in appearance with one another in response to the parallels of their life-styles. Again, the feathering of tiny coelurosaurs, while visible in only a few of their fossils, has been presumed in one or two cases as a logical extrapolation from available evidence.

Perhaps the dispute will never be resolved. In the meantime, however, the great popularity of dinosaurs among laymen invites more public input than is usual in scientific arguments. Such input is always welcome among conscientious scientists, for empirical science is fundamentally a democratic process open to all who choose to acquaint themselves with the data. Whatever its outcome, the controversy over dinosaur metabolism promises an enjoyable time for anyone involved.

ON TIME AND THE FOSSIL RECORD

In 1654, Archbishop James Ussher, Primate of the Anglican Church of Ireland, basing his calculations on the irrefutable word of God as revealed in Holy Scripture, announced that the universe was created at 9:00 a.m. on 26 October, four thousand and four years before the birth of Christ. Using the only authority known to his contemporaries in the European theological community, the archbishop sought, as humans always have, the limits of his world.

Today we continue Archbishop Ussher's search, but we now use a far more accurate source of information than his Bible. From the beginning of its history the earth has maintained a detailed geological journal, in which many important events of its life are recorded and can be examined by the more inquisitive and observant among its living forms. The translation of this journal has been simultaneously humbling and exalting. We have found that the earth is a far older and livelier place than Ussher and his comfortable British colleagues might have guessed, that Man the Wise and his few thousands of years of written history are temporal foam on a sea of thousands of *millions* of years. The very continents, we learn, skitter about and crash into one another over the earth's surface like pancakes on a hot greased griddle, wrinkling mighty mountain ranges into being and then sinking those mountains again beneath the ageless sea.

The gradual formation of the protoplanet earth from a rotating cloud of dust and gases seems to have occurred between 5000 million and 6000 million years ago. Since then the planet has remained essentially the same in structure, a ball of hot nickel-steel nearly 13,000 kilometers in diameter. A thin, cool film on the surface of this ball is composed of many other, mostly lighter, substances, solid, liquid, and gaseous, kept constantly stirred about by the heat of the

The approximate positions of the continents in relation to one another during the middle of the Mesozoic. The liveliness of earth's surface was unsuspected by early scientists.

nearby sun. Such a jumble of matter and energy, given enough time, is likely to form one or more changeable, self-replicating molecules that may be called "living." Luckily for us, it happened here.

The earliest traces of living systems appear in rocks some 3500 million years old. These oldest fossils represent blue-green algae and a multitude of bacteria-like forms. Such highly organized creatures suggest that life actually began some 500 million years earlier, making the lifestuff of earth some four billion years old.

Early algae combined water and carbon dioxide with bits of the sun's energy to power the living system. In this energy-trapping process, photosynthesis, they released vast quantities of molecular oxygen (O_2) into the seas and atmosphere. Oxygen is a substance so corrosive that it eats into iron and rock, a deadly poison to the life of the time. Between 600 million and 700 million years ago the concentration of oxygen at the earth's surface rose to such a degree that it began eliminating most of the living organisms on the young planet.

In response to this new threat, mutant forms appeared that were able not only to survive in oxygen but also to metabolize it in a process called respiration. These respiring organisms were so efficient in their use of energy that they were ultimately able to move from place to place in the pursuit of food. Relative latecomers in the earthly journal, they were the ancestors of all the *animals* that would inhabit the earth in aeons to come.

In our human urge to delimit and explain, we have sectioned the planetary journal into a number of arbitrary but useful chapters based on visible changes in the zoological record. Originally reflecting the history of animal life as perceived by several generations of geologists and paleontologists of many nationalities, the naming and spacing of these chapters often seem annoyingly

---

A "time tube," in which points in time are represented as disks perpendicular to the tube. The total length of the tube is six billion years, with the scale below equaling 100 million years. Using this scale, the tube is too long for the pages of this book, and so it has been bent upward at its more recent end to fit. It would take an electron microscope to discern Bishop Ussher's six thousand years on this scale.

Formation of planet   ⊢——⊣ 100 million years   Origin of life

capricious. However, they have become so ingrained in the terminology of science that it is best we use them here.

There are few undisputed fossils of animals more than 700 million years old, so the period from that time back to the beginning of earth history has been dubbed the Prepaleozoic Era, i.e., the era before the oldest animals. This vast time is succeeded by the Paleozoic Era, that of the oldest animals, which lasted 470 million years and is divided into seven periods of varying length, covering the early evolution of chordates and arthropods and the invasion of land by living systems.

After the oldest animals era comes that of the middle animals, the Mesozoic, the era with which we will be dealing in most of this book. The Mesozoic is marked by the triumph of the Archosauria, the class of advanced vertebrates including birds, dinosaurs, crocodilians, and certain other, extinct, animals, all descended from reptiles, and by their adaptive radiation into nearly every ecological niche available to advanced vertebrates. The Mesozoic, stretching from 230 million years ago to 65 million years ago, is divided into three periods ascending through time: the Triassic, Jurassic, and Cretaceous.

Lasting 45 million years, the Triassic period marks the diversification process in two important land vertebrate groups, the Archosauria and the Therapsida. By the beginning of the Jurassic, some 185 million years ago, the archosaurs had triumphed and the therapsids were extinct. Some therapsid descendants lived on, however, in the form of the first mammals, our Mesozoic ancestors.

The Jurassic era found the archosaurians consolidating their domination of the earth's land, producing forms to occupy most terrestrial niches available to land animals. During the Cretaceous, beginning 130 million years ago and lasting 65 million years, the archosaurs and the new flowering plants evolved side by side to produce some of the most progressive living things the world had ever seen.

Lasting in all 165 million years, the Mesozoic, by its enormous span, testifies to the success of the Archosauria, more specifically of the spectacular subclass Dinosauria, and marks one of the highest points of earthly evolution.

Something happened to end the Mesozoic, something so terrible that it

Family Hominidae, to which humans belong, originates on bottom of this disk

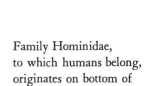

Cenozoic →
Cretaceous →
Jurassic →
Triassic →

Life emerges → onto land

Beginning of Paleozoic →

First animal → fossils

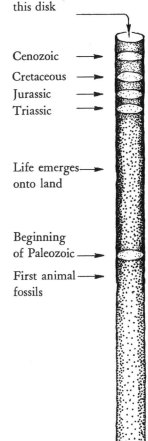

First fossils of bacteria and algae

swept most of the higher forms of life from the earth's land and seas. This worldwide death, about which we will speculate later in this book, was so extensive that the vertebrate world took several million years even to approximate its former glory, this time in the form not of archosaurs but of mammals like ourselves. Thus the era after the Mesozoic is called the Cenozoic, the era of the new animals. The Cenozoic is but 65 million years long so far, and we humans (in the broadest sense) occupy a scant two or three million of these. Such is true earthly time, a fair jump from the six thousand years imagined by good Bishop Ussher.

Our understanding of earth history is based largely on the fossil record. This record, while immeasurably rich and colorful, is not entirely democratic—it does not present a true cross section of the living forms of any particular era, particularly in the case of land dwellers. In order to become fossilized, a dead organism must remain in a recognizable condition despite exposure to the elements and to scavenging life forms. This happens in very few cases among the billions upon billions of animal deaths occurring daily, the scavengers being ever-hungry and the weather harsh. However, once in every few million deaths an organism, or a bit of one, becomes buried by water-carried mud or gravel, windblown sand, hot lava, or the like, and through thousands of years beneath the ground shares the gradual mineralization of its surroundings. In some cases organic matter from the organism is retained, coloring the resulting fossil or lending strength and texture to the remaining form, as in the case of coal, the fossilized organic matter of great primeval forests. Fossils may also take the form of burrows, tracks, and other traces of the activities of organisms during their lifetimes.

At any rate, fossilization nearly always requires the presence of liquid water, the agency usually inclined toward burying things. Because of this requirement, the fossil record of land animals is heavily biased in favor of those forms that were near water when they died. Thus the fossil record of the Mesozoic, for example, indicated to early paleontologists a moist, tropical or subtropical world characterized by swampy lowlands. This in turn suggested to them that the animals of the time were mainly the sorts that are confined to warm, wet places, and that these animals consequently exhibited a narrow range of specialization based on this sort of habitat.

We now know that during most of the Mesozoic the world was much as it is today, with ecological niches similar to those available in recent times. Although the watery bias continues to haunt the efforts of evolutionary biology, we are now aware that (for instance) many Mesozoic archosaurs, formerly relegated by paleontology to floating lazily about in stinking bogs, were actually swift upland dwellers who came down to drink, much as deer, wolves, and other mammals do today.

Another bias reflected in the fossil record is that of size. Because sturdy bones and other durable structures are more likely to survive millions of years of change in the earth's crust to become part of the collections in modern museums, the Mesozoic is popularly believed to have been an age of giants. There is also a certain public-relations bias among museum paleontologists toward giantism, for a truly monumental dinosaur skeleton is of more general interest than are many of the smaller animals with which the world has been populated. However, like other ecosystems before and after, the living system of the Mesozoic probably supported far more small animals, including tiny dinosaurs, than large ones. Their fossils are necessarily rare because of the relative fragility of these little animals; however, the number that have survived the aeons hints at the great diversity of small dinosaurs that once inhabited the planet.

Comparing the respective ways in which mammals and archosaurs have dominated terrestrial life is an adventure akin to paralleling the legend systems of chivalry and samurai. We humans are inclined to be partial toward life's drama as acted by our own class, Mammalia, in which we perceive the epitome of all life's beauty and grace. The Mesozoic world, however, presents the same ecologic play with foreign actors who, by their very outlandishness, introduce intriguing variation to the roles and ecologic niches with which we are already familiar.

GREAT FOSSIL LIZARDS

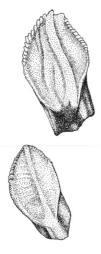

Fossil dinosaur teeth discovered by Mrs. Gideon Mantell and dubbed "iguana teeth" by her husband.

One day in March of 1822, Mrs. Gideon Mantell took a walk while her physician husband attended a patient outside the town of Lewes in Sussex, England. Mrs. Mantell had spent much of her adult life collecting fossils, and her trained eye fell on a large and most interesting tooth embedded in rock and having about it a patina of great age, as if its possessor had lived sometime before the Deluge with which the Creator was said in those days to have erased some of his errors. Dr. Mantell himself was an avid collector of fossils, and sparked by the finding of the tooth, he was able during subsequent months to find several more such teeth and some colossal bones in the area. It was quickly apparent to Mantell that the possessor of these bones and teeth was unlike any animal inhabiting Merry England in his own time, and furthermore, that he himself was incapable of assigning them an owner.

In those days there lived in France one Baron Georges Cuvier, a nobleman whose great learning had enabled him to keep his head through the social upheavals afflicting his nation and to become the foremost vertebrate anatomist of his time. Baron Cuvier had previously come into possession of a large fossil skull equipped with many fiercely hooked teeth. This specimen he correctly recognized as belonging to an immense extinct reptile related to the living monitor lizards. Mantell, acquainted with the baron's prowess in these matters, sent his fossil bones and teeth to Cuvier—who identified them as belonging to a hippopotamus and a rhinoceros respectively. The great man left Mantell unconvinced, however, and he appealed to other authorities with his specimens.

One of these was Mantell's old colleague Dean William Buckland, himself a paleontologist and Oxford Professor of Mineralogy and Geology. Dean Buckland had been doing a little fossil collecting of his own, gathering and examining certain huge bones and teeth discovered by workmen quarrying the Stones-field slates near Oxford. Much impressed by Baron Cuvier's extinct reptile, Dean Buckland decided that his specimens, also, must be lizard remains, and in 1824 he announced to the world the discovery of a "Megalosaurus or great fossil Lizard," which, by the evidence of its blade-shaped teeth, was a carnivore of no mean dimensions.

Buckland's great fossil lizard, however, did not influence him to disagree with Cuvier's hippo-rhino suggestions for the Mantell specimens. Still unconvinced, Mantell took his specimens to the Royal College of Surgeons in London, where the skulls of hundreds of vertebrates were maintained. Here he met one Samuel Stutchbury, naturalist and curator of the collection, who suggested that Mantell's fossil teeth resembled those of the living New World iguanas. Mantell finally agreed, and proudly publicized his discovery of yet another great fossil lizard, this one an herbivore named *Iguanodon*, "Iguana-tooth."

Megalosaurus and *Iguanodon* were the first of many such large extinct animals to be discovered in subsequent years. A brilliant young man named Richard Owen, Hunterian Professor to the Royal College of Surgeons, took it upon himself to analyze the accumulated fossil bones to produce a definitive statement on their nature. He observed that the remains of *Iguanodon, Megalosaurus,* and certain others shared characteristics otherwise separating them from the general run of reptilian skeletons (most notably in their possession of five vertebrae fused to the pelvic girdle). And so, on 2 August 1841, Owen publicly established a "distinct tribe or sub-order of Saurian Reptiles for which I would propose the name Dinosauria."

Dean Buckland's *Megalosaurus* bones were restored in this fashion for London's Crystal Palace exhibition. Compare this four-legged *Megalosaurus* with the modern restoration on p. 51.

Interestingly, these mighty animals, called by Owen the "crowns of reptilian creation," were used by him and other anti-evolutionists to counter the then-heretical views of the Frenchman Jean Baptiste Lamarck, who proposed that life may have proceeded from lower to more highly-organized forms through long periods of time. Owen suggested that if these majestic reptiles had indeed peopled the earth in distant times, their descendants, the lowly snakes and lizards of our own day, were evidence of some sort of retrograde evolution, if any at all. The concept of "evolution," therefore, was patent nonsense and deserved no credence among thinking men.

Creationists notwithstanding, the flow of more paleontological material to the world's museums and universities in following years began to suggest a distinct evolutionary progression among dinosaurs, easily traceable in time and indicating a series of species "births" and extinctions. The publication of Charles Darwin's monumental work *On the Origin of Species* in 1859 signaled the end of creationism and the advent of modern evolutionary biology. Offering to the world proof that evolution is due to the operation of environmental selection on myriad random mutations occurring in living forms, Darwin paved the way for a systematic paleontology based on the ecologic functions of animals and plants, their places in the environments of which they were part, and their positions on the evolutionary "tree."

Since then we have learned that the history of the dinosaurs and their relatives among the progressive Archosauria is one of splendid success and high evolutionary style. Indeed, the period of their ascendancy is greater than that of any other terrestrial vertebrate form, more than twice that of the mammals who followed them. During the whole of the Mesozoic there were mammals, our ancestors, but these were relegated to positions of ecologic insignificance by the victory of the dinosaurs, which, in retrospect, appears to have been the most important achievement of terrestrial vertebrates before the appearance of humans.

For as long as we have been aware of the existence of dinosaurs, we have perceived problems with the "great fossil Lizard" model in which they were trapped by early paleontology. This model was proposed, and stuck, largely because the archosaurs in general retain many of the bone structures of their reptilian forebears (much as mammals do), and gross bone structure was all the early paleontologists had to go on. However, their bone structure argued from the beginning that dinosaurs were something quite other than ordinary reptiles. Their posture, erect and fully bipedal as no lizard's could be, has always been a stumbling block to the "great fossil Lizard" proponents. In keeping with the lizard imagery of the times, early restorations often sadly distorted dinosaur structure to force upon the great skeletons a more "reptilian" conformation.

More recently, microscopic examination of dinosaur bone has revealed that this tissue is supplied with an extensive Haversian system, a network of canals supplying the bone structure with nourishment. A highly developed Haversian system indicates rapid metabolism of calcium and phosphorus (important ingredients of bone) and is suggestive of endothermy, "heating from within," the metabolic mode characteristic of "warm-blooded" animals. The implication, then, is that dinosaurs and some of their extinct relatives were very energetic animals similar metabolically to mammals.

This conclusion is enhanced by examination of the ratio between the total mass of predators in any environment and that of the herbivores on which they feed. In an ecologic system involving ectothermic ("heated from without") animals, those we have commonly and inaccurately called "cold-blooded," the predators require far less energy than do endothermic predators, with their high level of activity and internal heating systems. By counting the number of herbivores per carnivore in an assemblage ("fauna") of fossil bones, we can determine the number of vegetarians required to operate one predator. For instance, the number of small reptiles required to operate one big one is relatively small; the ratio of predators to herbivores in a reptile community may be as high as four to six. On the other hand, in a community of mammals the predator-prey ratio is usually less than one to twenty; dinosaur predator-prey ratios are consistently as low as or lower than those of mammals, implying a high metabolic rate for these animals. Of course, predator-prey ratios are mainly indicative of the metabolic rates of the predators themselves; nothing about the herbivores can be directly implied from such ratios. However, the fact that herbivorous dinosaurs descended from carnivorous ancestors that were very probably endotherms argues strongly that the herbivores were endotherms also. "Backward" evolution, i.e., from endothermy back to ectothermy, is an unlikely idea at best and perhaps a downright silly one, considering the postures and anatomies of the herbivorous dinosaurs.

Some of the more conservative modern paleontologists have attempted to discount predator-prey ratios as evidence for endothermy among dinosaurs. They use as their example the Komodo monitor, a large lizard inhabiting certain islands near Java. This predatory reptile, the largest of living lizards, is said to have a predator-prey ratio comparable to that of mammals even though it is very definitely an ectotherm. The Komodo monitor is a poor choice, however, for it is a declining species in an insular environment only recently populated by advanced mammals including humans. In addition to experiencing sharp competition from advanced predators such as dogs and cats, the Komodo monitor is also subject to depredations by human beings. Being large, interesting, edible, and easily captured, monitors end up all too often in stews or zoos, and the diminished numbers remaining are misinterpreted by some ecologists as proof of the natural bioenergetic conditions for these big lizards. Alas! What we see in the Komodo monitor is not a low predator-prey ratio but a fascinating animal in the process of extinction.

We are also confronted with the fact that mammals, known endotherms, coexisted with the earliest dinosaurs and might, because of their advanced metabolisms, be expected to have quickly superseded a race of great fossil lizards. However, for at least 140 million years of coexistence, the mammals were relegated by archosaurian success to marginal ecologic niches based on

---

A primitive "stem reptile," the Lower Permian *Limnoscelis*. From some such animal all reptiles, mammals, and archosaurs are descended.

small size, nocturnal ways of life, and an existence dependent on the sense of smell.

Finally, there is *size*; many great fossil lizard enthusiasts have suggested that dinosaurs regulated their temperatures "by being so large." It is proposed by these enthusiasts that the really enormous dinosaurs possessed surface areas (through which temperature changes occur) that were so small in proportion to their volumes that changes in body temperature were extremely slow. In addition, some have suggested that the Sauropoda, the true giants among dinosaurs, were simply too large to have fed themselves, given an endothermic metabolism. However, as we will see in the section devoted to these titans, they were actually superbly designed eating machines whose very breathing was subordinated to the constant passage of food down the gullet. And although it is true that some dinosaurs were giants, the majority were well within the size limits of modern mammals, many being as small as chickens. Great fossil lizard enthusiasts, in their attempts to base dinosaur metabolism on giantism,

are all too quick to forget this fact in their consideration of the question.

Nonetheless, for more than a century and a half the dinosaurs and their relatives have been maligned with epithets such as "reptilian" and "cold-blooded," gaining a reputation in popular culture for witless conservatism and inferior adaptability. In our ignorance of their unsurpassed success, we still often regard them as evolutionary dimbulbs doomed from the start by tiny brains and overgrown lizardlike physiques. Some of the leading paleontologists of our day perpetuate the pre-Darwinian views of Buckland and Mantell in their classification of dinosaurs as reptiles, and most of the rising generation of biologists remain trapped in that quagmire of scientific orthodoxy.

A few innovative people are taking another look at the Mesozoic, though, and in the process are accumulating evidence that dinosaur life was vastly different from what we have imagined in the past. In the pages that follow we

Reptiles

Therapsids/Mammals

Archosaurs

A graph of terrestrial econiches occupied by members of classes Reptilia, Therapsida/Mammalia, and Archosauria. The horizontal axis represents the passage of time; the vertical axis is a rough representation of the number of terrestrial econiches available to land-dwelling vertebrates. The early success of reptiles ended with the triumph of therapsids, which in their turn fell to the archosaurs. During the Cenozoic the mammals have occupied most terrestrial niches, archosaurs being relegated to the air (birds) and swamps (crocodilians) during this era.

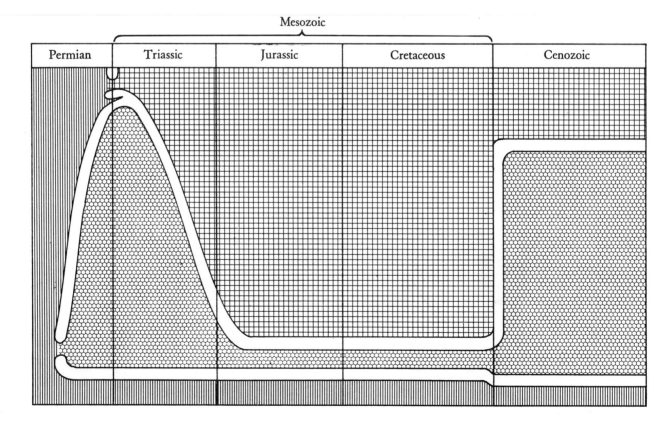

| Permian | Triassic | Jurassic | Cretaceous | Cenozoic |

will examine some of the new evidence, and, I hope, spread the controversy and kindle new interest in our splendid cousins the archosaurs. In the process we can also enhance our sense of the resilience and fragility that together are the beauty of life.

Much of this book is concerned with taxonomy, the art of classifying living beings into taxa or groups according to their places in the evolutionary process. These groups are arranged in order of descending size, which order is subject to considerable variation depending on the taxonomist doing the work. For instance, human beings are often classified thus:

TAXON	NAME	DESCRIPTION
Kingdom	Animalia	Animals, as opposed to plants, bacteria, etc.
Phylum	Chordata	Animals that, at some point in their lives, are equipped with a notochord, a stiffening rod running the length of the body.
Subphylum	Vertebrata	Chordates equipped with a bony or cartilaginous set of vertebrae protecting the main nerve cord.
Class	Mammalia	Vertebrates feeding their young with milk from mammary glands.
Subclass	Eutheria	Mammals equipped with placentae, with which the young are nourished *in utero*.
Order	Primates	Generalized eutherians with five-fingered hands and feet usually equipped with nails instead of claws.
Suborder	Anthropoidea	Advanced "manlike" primates with forward-directed vision and large brains.
Superfamily	Hominoidea	Larger anthropoids with forelimbs specialized for brachiation or manipulation.
Family	Hominidae	Bipedal, largely predatory anthropoids that hunt with weapons held in the forelimbs.
Genus	*Homo*	"Human" hominids.
Species	*sapiens*	"Wise" humans, i.e., those who picked this name.

As an example of variation in the taxonomist's art, it may be noted that the suborder Anthropoidea, above, is also sometimes considered a "superfamily." Taxonomists may include various other additional groupings such as tribes, cohorts, subfamilies, and so forth, some of which will appear later in this book.

In spite of its shortcomings, taxonomy is a useful evolutionary shorthand indicating at a glance an organism's history and characteristics. Because it is an art practiced in many nations, taxonomy is conducted in a blend of scientific neo-Latin with an admixture of Greek roots designed to span modern linguistic barriers in order that workers in all parts of the world may conveniently compare data. In the case of extinct animals such as those appearing in this book, the Latinisms of taxonomy are all we have for names; and while such monikers as *Hypsilophodon*, *Coelophysis*, and *Parasaurolophus* may seem unwieldy at first glance, they are the most convenient for our purposes. To ease the use of these multisyllabic handles, I have provided a little glossary at the back of the book.

REPTILES PAST AND PRESENT

Since the early paleontologists pegged dinosaurs with a reptilian structure and mode of life, it is interesting to examine true reptiles, to see where they fit into the evolutionary scheme of things and to compare them with what we know of archosaurian biology. Reptiles, especially the living species, are subject to much vilification through misinformation, and it may do both us and them some good to try to straighten out their public image.

The place of origin of all life is in the water, and the story of the invasion of land by living beings is a story of water carrying; water is the solvent in which the processes of life are conducted, and in the terrestrial environment, organisms must provide themselves with this solvent to continue their metabolizing and reproducing. Thus when vertebrates, in the form of fish, first left their watery home for the rigors of dry-land living, they were still chained to liquid water. Although forced by uneven water supplies to adapt to breathing air and to terrestrial locomotion, these first land colonists continued for many millions of years to lay their eggs in water. The process of mating was external; the male released his sperm into water simultaneously with the release of the female's eggs, and in the open water the eggs were fertilized and hatched. In this fashion the young, beginning as immature larvae, developed in the manner of fish for a time before returning to land; thus these primitive terrestrial vertebrates are called amphibians, from Greek roots meaning "two-lived."

Around 300 million years ago some of these land-dwelling pioneers were able to break the reproductive link with open water by perfecting a mechanism whereby eggs might be fertilized while still inside the female, rather than floating free in water. This is not as great a step as it may seem, for most amphibians mate in a very close embrace in the water to ensure maximum contact between sperm and eggs. In areas where open water was shallow or periodically absent there was a selective advantage for animals whose eggs could remain within the moist interior of the female during fertilization. She might then be able to carry these fertile eggs for a time, until she found suitable water or other moisture in which to release them.

It remained for the first reptiles to evolve an egg that carried its own water, in the form of amniotic fluid. This amniote egg is simply a tiny portable pond in which the amphibian egg may develop, contained by an enclosing membrane called the amnion. Later in its evolution the amniote egg was enclosed by a shell, which further protected it, not only from moisture loss but from crushing by gravity. The addition of a large nourishing yolk permitted the growing larva, now called an embryo, to reach an advanced stage of development, so that most newborn reptiles are able to care for themselves at birth.

By evolving these little self-contained ponds, the vertebrates broke from their reproductive dependence on open water and became true land dwellers. The amniote egg persists not only in reptiles but in their descendants the archosaurs and mammals. In the latter class the shell is usually lost and the developing embryo is retained for even longer within its mother, eliminating the stage in which the egg is a separate and highly vulnerable unit. The amnion persists in mammals, however, and in the higher forms becomes part of the elegant placenta through which the youngster is nourished directly by the mother without requiring a large yolk.

Revamping the reproductive cycle was only one of a number of changes forced on the vertebrates in their quest for mastery of the terrestrial environment. A water-dwelling animal is protected from desiccation by his environment; however, if exposed to the air he will quickly lose moisture through his skin, ultimately dying if he is unable to regain the water. During the early part of their experimentation with terrestrial living, the vertebrates experimented with a variety of skin coverings, such as the heavy mucous coatings that compose the "slime" of frogs and salamanders, designed to reduce the drying menace and permit them to carry their internal water safely about in dry environments.

Reptiles are covered with a dry skin surface, usually composed of scales, insulating their moist interior from desiccation by air. The evolution of dry skin was a major step in the conquest of land by vertebrates.

Early amphibians spent much of their time soaking about in swamps, but when these bodies of water dried up in response to the vagaries of climate, they were forced to go without for a time. Selective pressure ultimately resulted in the evolution of a dry, relatively lifeless body boundary, the *stratum corneum* or horn layer, protecting the moist interior from the hostile exterior. Characteristic of this integument is the protein *keratin*, a hard, flexible substance abundant in horn, claws, hooves, hair, and the scales of reptiles and their descendants. Thus reptiles, with their layer of scales, are far from slimy—in fact they are drier to the touch than most mammals or birds.

Our new reptile, living perhaps 265 million years ago, is now ready to refine his act and more fully exploit the world of dry land. One problem of terrestrial living is variability in temperature. Any animal's metabolism is most efficient within a narrow range of temperatures, perhaps five degrees Centigrade at most. Amphibians tend to operate at temperatures commensurate with those of the waters in which they were born, and reptiles at temperatures somewhat higher; the latter gain their heating directly from the sun and are thus permitted a higher level of activity than their amphibian forebears. However, while bodies of water hold heat well and change temperature slowly, air holds heat hardly at all, and the mere passing of the sun behind a cloud may cause a temperature drop of several degrees. The temperatures at which most modern terrestrial reptiles function most efficiently are between 33° and 38° Centigrade, comparable to our own normal temperature. Thus the term "cold-blooded" when used in reference to reptiles is highly inaccurate. A reptile whose blood is cold is an inefficiently functioning, nearly helpless reptile, easy prey for any predator happening along. Thus most reptiles anticipating cold tend to hide themselves away, burrowing into the ground or otherwise making themselves less available before they are forced into a state of cold-induced inactivity.

The physiology of the new reptile is still close to that of his amphibian ancestors, who regulated their temperatures by staying in or near water. Unfortunately, however, having taken to wandering about in the uplands, the poor reptile has no such easy recourse to water when the air temperature changes. If the temperature rises too far, he may go into convulsions and die in the sun; if it drops, as at night, he grinds to a halt, remaining inactive where he stands until touched again by the sun. During the early ages of reptilian evolution, animals lucky enough to wake up in the sun early in the day might wander about snapping up their still-torpid cousins who chanced to lie longer in the shade. Thus a strong selective pressure arose for some form of temperature regulation in order that the early reptiles might maintain themselves at optimum operating temperatures as much of the time as possible. Because a reptile's temperature, like that of an amphibian, is dependent on external conditions, we call him an ectotherm, which, as we have seen, means that he is "heated from without."

There are a number of ways in which such an animal may regulate its temperature. The easiest of these is behavioral—the animal takes care to be in the right place at the right time to govern its body heat. When overheated, such an animal seeks a *heat sink*, a cool place in which it may "sink" some of its excess heat. This heat sink may take the form of shade, or cool subsurface earth or the like—it is simply an environment cooler than the animal seeking it. When too cool for comfort the same animal seeks a *heat source*, such as the sun, warm rocks, or what have you. The familiar dead snake on the warm highway on summer evenings is a victim of the impulse to seek a heat source after sunset.

Early reptiles improved their heat-control behavior with a variety of techniques observable among their living reptilian descendants. For instance, gaining one's temperature from outside requires an integument that readily transmits heat, which is why reptiles are never insulated by hair or feathers. In addition, many of them are able to change the shade, and therefore the heat-absorbing qualities, of their skin. A hot horned-lizard of the genus *Phrysonoma* becomes pale in order to reflect the sun's energy, while the same animal when cool darkens his color in order to absorb more heat energy. The diameter of

blood vessels in the skin may also vary, dilating to carry more blood to the surface for heat exchange or constricting to reduce the exchange. Such changes in blood vessel diameter are called vasomotor adjustments and persist in mammals and birds—if you run for a while and heat up, you become red in the face as your surface capillaries pass excess heat to the surrounding air.

Reptiles also use accessory heat-control systems such as evaporation; when water evaporates from a surface, it takes heat with it, cooling that surface in the process. Overheated reptiles sometimes pant, evaporating water from the inner surfaces of their lungs in order to provide cooling. Cold reptiles may warm up by releasing metabolic energy through muscle activity; certain snakes,

---

In a bleak Permian landscape, the fantastic solar-heat-collecting pelycosaur *Dimetrodon* prepares to snap up a less efficient cousin. Pelycosaurs were early representatives of the reptilian line that ultimately led to the first mammals.

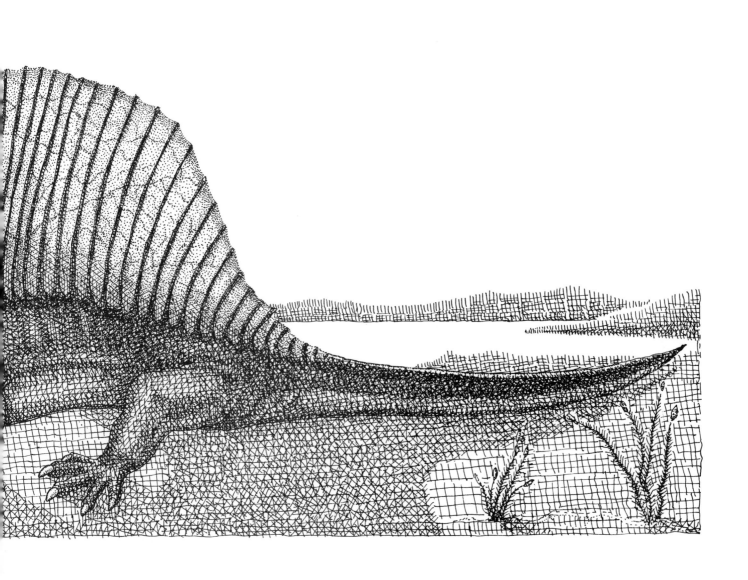

The pariesaur *Scutosaurus* was a reptile whose body temperature was maintained by a low surface/volume ratio.

for instance, are able to raise their body temperatures a few degrees by rapidly contracting body muscles in a process akin to shivering. A large lizard may do the same in the process of simply running.

Increase in size is another method of stabilizing body temperature, one that works especially well in climates where temperature rarely drops far below a reptile's optimum operating temperature. A large animal has less surface per unit volume for gaining or losing heat and once having reached optimum temperature is often able to maintain it with less difficulty than a small animal in the same environment.

Finally, of course, there is the old recourse to water with its relatively stable temperatures. As the early reptiles increased in diversity and success, many of them returned to an aquatic existence, some becoming true marine forms in the process.

As you can see, temperature control is quite a sticky problem for reptiles. During the Permian period, 265 to 230 million years ago, when the reptiles were undergoing a great adaptive radiation across the planet, there was much experimentation with modes of temperature control. Each tiny advance in the competition for even and efficient body temperature brought its possessor an advantage in the evolutionary arena and perchance the ability to exploit newer, uncontested environments. Some of this experimentation approached the bizarre in its outward manifestations, as in the case of certain pelycosaurs who evolved a system of solar heating based on large heat-collecting sails supported on elongated vertebral spines. Turning this sail across the rays of the morning sun, a pelycosaurian predator could quickly heat up and set off on the day's search for prey while its relatives slept on unaware.

Some reptiles, being too slow to escape their predatory relatives, specialized in the evolution of protective armor. So successful were they that their descendants, the familiar turtles and tortoises, have persisted relatively unchanged across the hundreds of millions of years of their existence. Others, taking the route toward large size and small surface area, became the nearly globular pariesaurs. These immense masses of flesh moved slowly about on stubby legs, protected by size from most predators and perhaps internally heated to some degree by their vast and unspeakable digestive processes.

Some early reptiles took advantage of smaller size to occupy microniches in

---

The ichthyosaurs were reptiles who returned to a marine existence in order to rely on stable ocean temperatures for regulation of body heat. They occupied an ecologic niche approximating that of advanced sharks, which replaced them toward the end of the Cretaceous, and probably resembled dolphins in life.

which they might persist unnoticed by larger predators. Those small forms lived in a manner analogous to our living lizards, moving quickly from heat source to heat sink and preying on the insects and other small animals of their time.

Those reptiles that returned to an aquatic existence, with its promise of equable temperatures and ease of movement, diversified into as many forms as there were watery niches to support them. Some became animated clam-rakes, the ecologic equivalents of the modern mollusk-eating walrus. Others stuck to the swamps, leading an amphibious existence based on the eating of their amphibian neighbors and whatever land reptiles were unwary enough to approach their powerful jaws.

Still others took to the open sea, becoming great fast predators on the fish of the time. Mosasaurs, such as the great lizard described by Baron Cuvier, were seagoing reptiles up to ten meters long with double-hinged jaws capable of an awesome gape. Plesiosaurs, animals resembling the fabled Orm of Loch Ness, snapped up fish with their long, agile necks, while ichthyosaurs ("fish-lizards") paralleled the form of fish in their quest for oceangoing protein and became reptilian analogues of the dolphins of our own times. Such animals were completely unable to return to land and took to bearing their young alive in the sea.

The Permian was the true Age of Reptiles, during which most of the earth's surface was invaded by these interesting animals. Using various combinations of the heat-control systems available to them, Permian reptiles assumed many baroque and anomalous forms, which continue to delight and amaze their human descendants 230 million years later. All in all, however, the reptiles never really achieved effective temperature control independent of external heat sources and sinks. Because of this inadequacy they were (and are) forced to spend a large part of their existence in an inactive state, and much of their active life is spent in seeking environmental temperatures suitable to their needs of the moment. In addition, the three-chambered reptilian heart, continuing as a relic of amphibian days, remains somewhat inefficient in that it permits the mixing of "spent" blood from the body with "new," oxygen-rich blood from the lungs, so that a reptile is never able to enjoy complete oxygenation of its body tissues. This deficiency is reflected in the fact that reptiles' legs are shorter per unit mass than those of comparable mammals and birds, so that their possessors spend most of their lives sitting on their stomachs. This arrangement results in a mode of locomotion that can best be described as a waddle, and reptiles are never able to attain any running speed for more than a few feet. The Permian was an age of slow motion.

ARCHOSAURIA

As we have seen, some Permian reptiles adopted a freshwater existence based on predation in relatively shallow waters. Frequenting rivers and lakes, where they captured fish or land reptiles that approached the water too closely, these animals continued to come ashore to bask in the sun and to lay eggs. Their amphibious life-style forced some changes in form and physiology, changes that prepared them for the foundation of the mighty class Archosauria.

Technical classifications offer many minute skeletal peculiarities by which we may identify archosaurs, but in this book we will describe them as a group of related vertebrates descended from crocodilelike forms, whose teeth (when present) grow in sockets (rather than being welded to the jaw, as in lizards) and whose circulatory and nervous systems share certain progressive characteristics not present in reptiles.

Our prearchosaurian freshwater predators looked and lived rather like crocodiles, the most primitive living archosaurians and a group representing the perfection of the amphibious freshwater predatory way of life. So precisely do crocodilians fit this niche that they have occupied it virtually unchanged and unchallenged since their appearance around 200 million years ago, and there is little doubt that their resemblance to the lost archosaur ancestor is strong. In taking a close look at the living crocodilians we gain a glimpse into the circumstances surrounding the birth of the Archosauria.

Crocodilians, including alligators and gavials as well as true crocodiles, are all amphibious; that is, they all spend part of their time in water and part on land. The water-dwelling life, of course, is secondary; these animals are descended from fully terrestrial reptiles and bear the stamp of their ancestry. In reverting to the water, crocodilians have changed their shape to facilitate

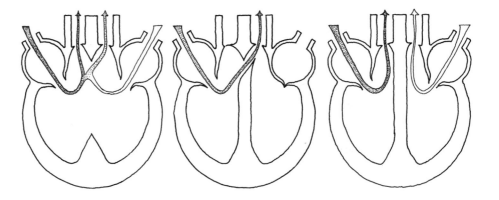

Diagrams of hearts of (*left*) reptile, (*middle*) crocodile, and (*right*) a fully endothermic archosaur such as a dinosaur or bird. Arrows show the passage of blood through the hearts; shaded portions of arrows indicate "spent" or CO_2-laden blood returning from the body. The reptile heart permits mixing of "spent" blood with "fresh" oxygen-rich blood from the lungs, preventing really efficient oxygenation of the body tissues, while the double-pump heart at right corrects this deficiency. The crocodile heart is shown in its submerged position, with blood bypassing the lungs. On land, the valve in the center wall of this heart is closed.

---

efficient swimming; the tail is long and strong, a sculling implement for fast movement through the water. In addition, the hind legs, used to change direction with a kick on the bottom and also to propel the animal rapidly out of the water to snag terrestrial prey, tend to be more powerful and longer than the forelegs. This fact is of great significance, for these strong hind legs set the foundation for the bipedal walk that was to launch the archosaurian conquest of the terrestrial world.

Because their eggs are left on land even though the parents spend so much of their time in the water, crocodilians show advanced parental behavior that is unknown among reptiles. Rather than leaving her eggs completely unprotected, the female (and in some cases the male) remains on land during the incubation period of the eggs, which she carefully buries and near which she remains until hatching time, when the young cry from within their eggs. On hearing the tiny chirps, the parent digs the young out of the nest and carries them to the water (compare this with the reptile's burying the eggs and abandoning them to their fate), where she washes them off and remains with them for the next two months or so until they are large enough to escape most predators. During this period of parental protection the father assists in defending a territory against invaders, while attempting to keep the young in sight. If a young crocodile is caught by a predator, it cries out in alarm, rather like the cheeping of a young bird, and its parents and other adult crocodiles rush toward the sound. Meanwhile all other young within hearing distance head for cover.

Social behavior of equal complexity is seen in the lives of adult crocodiles, which may cooperate in the hunt, driving fish before them in groups and sharing the catch. Land animals too big to be dragged to the water are often divided on land in an amicable fashion, or even carried by more than one crocodile. There is a definite dominance order among male crocodiles, assuring each his place in the society of adults. In addition, each adult male maintains a territory for the mating and breeding season. Naturally, all of this social behavior is reflected in a brain considerably more advanced in structure than that of reptiles, and it is logical to assume that brain changes of this sort were occurring in ancestral archosaurs.

Crocodiles have perfected the sit-and-wait method of hunting that is necessary for success in fishing, as any angler will know. Not only may they sit in shallow water with only nostrils, eyes, and ears protruding from the surface, but they may also sink to the bottom to lurk in the vegetation in wait for fish and other prey. To permit a longer wait, they possess modified circulatory systems involving an improved distribution of oxygen to body tissue. The crocodile, when breathing, possesses a true four-chambered heart in which freshly oxygenated blood from the lungs is completely separated from the "spent" blood returning from the body. Thus with a very few breaths the croc

---

A comparison of the resting stances of reptiles (*left*) and archosaurs. Arrows show the respective angles of stability of these classes, angles constructed with apexes at the animals' centers of gravity and rays to the feet. The narrow angle of stability of archosaurs reflects the constant activity of the leg muscles required to hold the animal aloft, activity which produces a good deal of heat even when the animal is at rest.

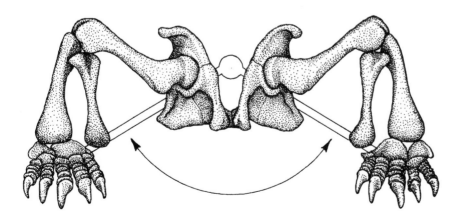
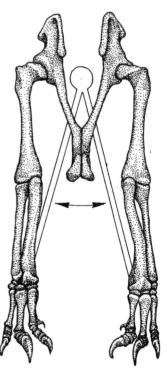

may store up a good deal of oxygen, then sink to the bottom and wait. During the often extended period of submerged lurking, the animal is able to bypass the lungs by opening an accessory valve in the wall between the ventricles of its heart. This remarkable system represents a submarine return to the reptilian heart, conserving oxygen that might otherwise have been wasted on the non-functioning lungs and lengthening the period the animal may spend on the bottom. In addition, the efficient four-chambered heart of the breathing crocodile allows the animal the extra oxygen required during its extended nest-guarding and other terrestrial activities and aids in the operation of the animal's comparatively advanced brain and social behavior.

Euparkeria, an early African archosaur, probably moved on all fours most of the time; however, it was capable of short bursts of speed on two legs.

True crocodilians did not appear until the Mid-Triassic, but there is little reason to believe that their late-Permian ancestors were very different from them in appearance or life-style. During the early Triassic, however, the world experienced a drying trend that reduced the number of comfortable swamps available to the earliest archosaurs. Those that were able to remain successfully in water are represented today by crocodilians. Most others died out, but those who survived the forced return to land did so, paradoxically, by capitalizing on the above-discussed adaptations to water-dwelling.

Through the advantages conferred by their long hind legs and new hearts, early terrestrial archosaurs were able to achieve far more agility and speed than their reptilian contemporaries. One group, called thecodonts or "socket-teeth," began a process of refinement of locomotion and energy use to gain maximum advantage in the competition for land space. An early step in the

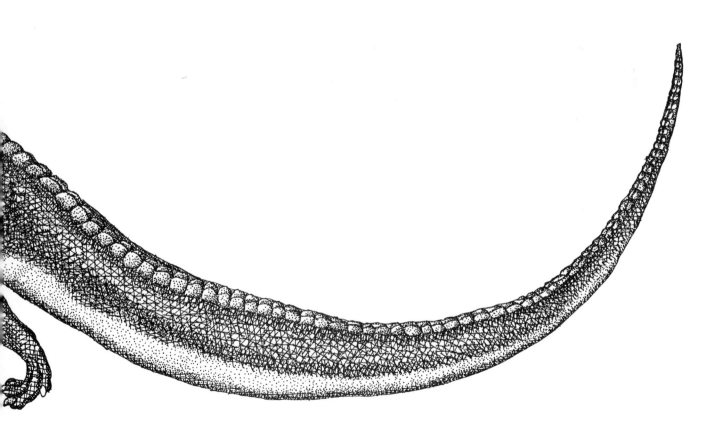

improvement of the terrestrial archosaur system came in the arrangement of the hind legs in thecodonts. Already developed for power, these legs gradually swung in beneath the body, supporting more of its mass and contrasting its posture sharply with the splayed stance of reptiles. This change in posture, from a lizardlike resting on the belly to the archosaurian "fixed pillar" position, was aided by the structure of the heart. Raising the body off the ground naturally requires the expenditure of more energy than is needed in a belly-on-the-ground posture, and the expenditure of more energy in an animal requires the consumption of more oxygen.

A reasonable example of an early, partially erect thecodont seems to be *Euparkeria*, a small form whose adults measured about a meter in length. Retaining a row of large bony plates along its back from its crocodilelike ancestors, this animal is classed in the suborder Pseudosuchia, "paracrocodiles," giving a general idea of its appearance. *Euparkeria* moved on all fours when walking slowly, but it had the option of rearing onto its long and highly developed hind legs for a sprint, freeing the forelegs, with which it may have knocked insects out of the air. The insects were the fastest animals in the early Triassic and may have been the incentive for *Euparkeria's* pioneering tendency toward high-speed living.

Through the millennia the process continued, the gradually straightening hind legs and the evolving double heart enhancing each other's progress until at some momentous point, forever lost in time, the separation of the heart halves was complete and the thecodont posture was fully bipedal. That this was accomplished fairly early in the Triassic we know by the presence in the Mid-Triassic of thecodonts whose bones indicate a completely bipedal structure and the capability for great speed. The forelegs are reduced to grasping organs and must have been only minimally useful should the animal have attempted a four-legged gait. Because of their light, bipedal builds, these thecodonts are

---

Ornithosuchus was a form transitional between more primitive archosaurs and the first dinosaurs and appears to have been fully bipedal.

known collectively as the family Ornithosuchidae ("bird-crocodiles"), a representative example of which is the genus *Saltoposuchus*, the appropriately named "leaping crocodile" of Triassic Europe. This was a speedy carnivore a bit more than a meter in length, whose long tail balanced the shorter body in lever fashion with the fulcrum located at the acetabulum, the "vinegar-cup" or pelvic hollow in which the femur (thighbone) rotates.

Now, such erect posture radically changes the requirements placed on the muscles of the hind leg. In order to stand or walk upright, an animal must tense the muscles straightening the legs, and this tension must be maintained for as long as the animal is standing. In an animal so constructed that its standing posture raises its center of gravity far off the ground, a great deal of constant activity is required of the muscle masses about the joints of legs and limb girdles. This activity is called muscle tone, and like all animal metabolic processes, it releases heat. Thus the changes in muscular organization involved in adopting the "fixed pillar" posture caused the animal's system to produce heat even at rest. Once their posture and circulation permitted this internal heating, thecodonts had crossed the border to endothermy and the way was clear for their exploitation of the earth's surface independent of temperature considerations.

It remained for the first fully erect, fully oxygenated, internally heated archosaurs to capitalize on their new metabolic systems and develop sophisticated control over their temperatures, eliminating the possibility of overheating and, in cool weather, remaining warm enough to prevent collapse. Fast-moving *Saltoposuchus* must have panted like a reptile to dissipate excess heat. Archosaurs enhanced the cooling efficiency of their panting by evolving a system of air sacs extending through the body. This system, which also lightened the animals considerably, was highly developed in the giant sauropods and persists in birds, dinosaur descendants. In addition, *Saltoposuchus* probably possessed a skin surface that readily transmitted heat, an inheritance from its reptilian ancestors. A bit of improvement of the vasomotor system in the skin probably gave such animals all the cooling capability they needed in most warm environments.

The handling of cold was quite another matter. In equable climates the newly endothermic thecodonts may simply never have encountered intense cold, but where there was much variation in temperature, selective pressure was intense toward some system of protecting the warmth of the body. In small thecodonts, whose surface area was large in comparison with their volume, the old heat-transmitting reptilian skin was a liability in any but the most even climate and was forced to undergo some process of insulation if the animals were to survive. It seems reasonable to suppose that early endothermic thecodonts evolved some mechanism for trapping "dead air" next to the skin for prevention of heat loss, a mechanism which would also permit air circulation should the animal overheat. Although such a mechanism would be composed of soft tissue and thus unlikely to survive in fossils, we are graced by fate in having a delicately preserved little thecodont, *Longisquamata* ("long-scales") of Mid-Triassic Russia, showing evidence of having possessed scales modified to insulate the body's surface. These keeled and elongated scales overlapped one another, trapping air pockets between themselves and the skin; to cool the animal they might be erected to allow dissipation of excess heat.

Refinement of this insulating technique among the Archosauria finally led to

---

Longisquamata, a Triassic archosaur with overlapping scales of a sort possibly ancestral to feathers. The structure on the animal's back was probably a territorial display device used much as is the large tail on a tom turkey.

the evolution of true feathers, which are just such keeled scales frayed at the edges to trap yet more air. Although the history of these delicate structures is necessarily sparse, we are treated by the fossil record to a few preserved scales of the primitive Triassic archosaur *Ornithosuchus* already indicating a tendency toward an air-trapping body covering. The scales in these animals were far longer than broad and had a central rib from which grooves or rays passed to the edges of the scales. There is but a short evolutionary jump, probably, from this point to the appearance of real feathers; and we know that by Mid-Jurassic times true feathers were present among small dinosaurs, feathers that show clearly in fossils preserved in the finest lithographic limestones and shales of the times. *Archaeopteryx lithographica*, a little coelurosaur to be treated with its order later in this book, was fully insulated with contour feathers so similar to those of modern birds that the discoverers of these beautiful fossils insisted that they must actually be birds, hence the name *Archaeopteryx*, "old wing." Similarly well preserved pterosaurs (archosaurs specialized for flight on flaps of skin between wingtip and body) show a full covering of hair, another efficient insulator. These hair and feather body coats argue, by their complexity and specialization, a long prior evolutionary history for such elegant structures among the Archosauria.

It is during the Triassic that we first begin to locate traces of the remarkable archosaurians collectively known as dinosaurs, direct descendants of pseudo-suchian thecodonts. Indeed, such transitional forms as *Ornithosuchus*, the "bird-crocodile" of Upper Triassic Scotland, have been variously classed as pseudo-suchians and dinosaurs of the infraorder Carnosauria. Whatever else they were, *Ornithosuchus* and its ilk were fleet-footed, fast metabolizing, and probably efficiently insulated where necessary. No longer did temperature stand in their way, and by the end of the Triassic many genera of dinosaurs, fully and successfully endothermic, were going about the business of conquering the continents of Earth. They were the most progressive living things on the planet to date and would continue so, unchallenged, for another 120 million years.

DINOSAURS

Ask a properly stodgy professor of paleontology what a dinosaur is, and he'll probably tell you that there is no such thing. He'll tell you that the Mesozoic vertebrate land fauna was dominated by two suborders of the order Archosauria of class Reptilia: Saurischia ("lizard-hips") and Ornithischia ("bird-hips"). He *won't* tell you that these groups are composed of descendants of the bipedal endothermic thecodonts who dominated because of their advanced metabolic and postural systems, for he doesn't believe in endothermic thecodonts and he persists in calling all archosaurs "cold-blooded reptiles."

To simplify this book, however, and to point up our concern with archosaurian metabolic sophistication, we will speak of the dinosaurs as a subclass, Dinosauria, of a class, Archosauria, including all those progressive forms that, descending from thecodonts, improved on the old reptilian heart and headed toward endothermy. Some never made it to full endothermy, including our friends the crocodiles and a host of extinct forms. The dinosaurs, however, appear to have been fully endothermic, thus meriting at least a subclass of their own. This is not an arbitrary reclassification of my own but is based on a suggestion made by R. T. Bakker and P. M. Galton as long ago as 1974 that it would be more sensible to place vertebrates in classes in accordance with their metabolic structures rather than to classify them according to superficial skeletal similarities. Although not yet accepted in many zoological circles, this novel classification is certainly simpler for our present purposes.

The earliest preserved dinosaurs, excluding *Ornithosuchus* and other transitional forms, were members of the order Saurischia, those dinosaurs possessing a triradiate hip structure somewhat reminiscent of that found in lizards. This resemblance is superficial, however, for the saurischian hip is a highly special-

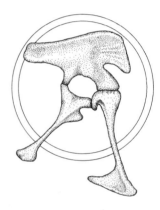

The triradiate saurischian hip, which occurs in coelurosaurs, carnosaurs, and sauropods.

ized structure facilitating true bipedal walking, an impossibility for reptiles. Among the Saurischia are two suborders, Theropoda and Sauropoda, "beast-feet" and "lizard-feet" respectively—"beast-feet" because theropods had four or fewer toes on the hind feet, like many specialized mammals; "lizard-feet" because sauropods had five toes, like lizards. The earlier and less specialized of these, the suborder Theropoda, includes bipedal forms that represent all of the carnivorous dinosaurs throughout the Mesozoic Era plus some interesting primitive forms transitional to the Sauropoda. From an Ornithosuchus-like progenitor, theropods appeared during the Mid-Triassic and quickly radiated into a variety of ecologic niches suited to predators of all sizes, retaining for the most part the ancestral patterns of rapid bipedal locomotion based on a

An "ecogram" showing the Mesozoic terrestrial ecologic niches dominated by Archosauria. Only birds and crocodiles survived the end of the era. In this diagram the crocodiles, never fully terrestrial, are not shaded.

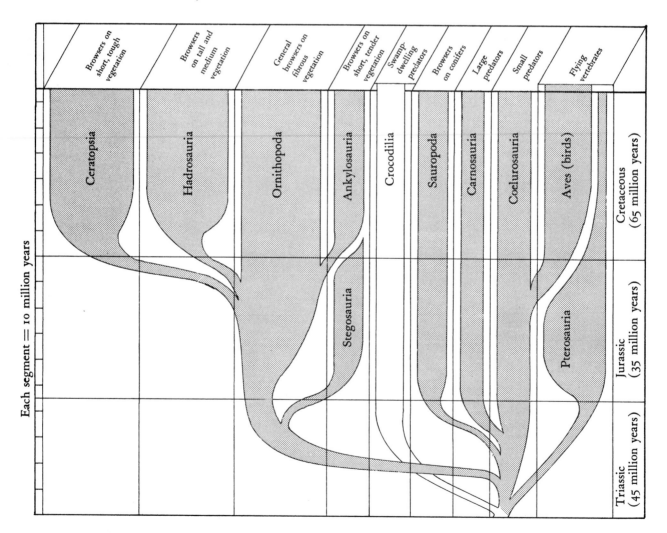

hollow-boned birdlike frame. Although this tendency is already seen in the thecodont *Euparkeria*, by the late Triassic the theropods had diversified into three infraorders, Coelurosauria and Carnosauria, representing smaller and larger predators respectively, and Prosauropoda, aberrant herbivorous forms.

Some of the earliest indisputable dinosaurs are members of infraorder Coelurosauria—light, fast hollow-boned predators who occupied ecological niches similar to those of the lesser cats of today. The delicacy and openness of their skeletal structure is reflected in the name of the group, meaning "lizards with hollows." That the little coelurosaurs were highly successful predators from the start is shown by the fact that they diversified into at least three families by the end of the Triassic and six and possibly more families during the course of the Mesozoic.

A typical early coelurosaur is the aptly named *Saltopus* ("leaping-foot") from Europe of Mid-Triassic times. *Saltopus* embodies all the design elements that were to make later coelurosaurs so successful. The "neckless," primitive condition of *Ornithosuchus* and its cousins was superseded in *Saltopus* by the evolution of a long and highly mobile neck bearing a light, wedge-shaped head with sharp teeth and large orbits mounting undoubtedly acute eyes. The forelimbs still bore five fingers, a condition primitive in dinosaurs, but these "hands" were useless in locomotion and were adapted for grasping the agile little hunter's prey. The spine, from shoulder to tip of tail, was stiffened by sturdy ligaments, so that the structure of *Saltopus* was relatively rigid. This condition provided stability in the leverlike posture of the animal but required little expenditure of energy to hold the body rigid and entirely off the ground, since the limber neck compensated for loss of flexibility in the rest of the body.

Old restorations show *Saltopus* and similar animals in an interesting "fossil Lizard" position. Since the bones indicate that the animal could never have walked on all fours like a lizard, paleontologists who believed dinosaurs to be reptiles were forced to arrange them as *tripods*, with the tail dragging behind to help support the animal's slow, painful progress on its hind legs!

These hind legs are the most impressive part of *Saltopus*. The femur (thighbone) was shorter than the tibia and fibula (shinbones), so that the walking stroke must have involved a short, swift rearward femoral swing accented by a far longer swing of the shin, a condition indicative of great speed in running. In addition, the carpal (instep) bones were highly elongated, effectively producing yet another limb segment to further lengthen the stride. Muscles on the back of the calf caused this long foot to snap back with tremendous force against the ground with each step, for *Saltopus* was really more a runner than a leaper. The addition of such an auxiliary limb segment is

an evolutionary ploy of almost all endothermic vertebrates that specialize in high speed, such as cheetahs, horses, and large running birds, and is not present in living ectotherms.

Saltopus stood only about twenty centimeters high at the hips and weighed about a kilogram (or about two pounds). This superb little predator parallels in structure its cousin and probable descendant the roadrunner of southwestern North America. Such parallelism indicates that its ecologic niche was probably similar to that of the bird, certainly excluding *Saltopus* from the ranks of the "cold-blooded." Because it was so small and metabolically "fast," *Saltopus*

was probably insulated with some form of the feather-scale discussed earlier, and all in all must have been quite a handsome and efficient little animal.

As noted previously, a host of different coelurosaurs evolved from some *Saltopus*-like ancestor. Later Triassic genera include the famous *Coelophysis,* a large number of which were found in one small deposit near Abiquiu, New Mexico. Although a good deal larger than *Saltopus*, being about a meter high at the hip, *Coelophysis* is built on the same general plan with a few refinements. The hand of *Saltopus* had five fingers; these have been reduced in number to four in *Coelophysis*, with the fourth much reduced in size. The three remaining digits are much enlarged, the first being slightly opposed to the other two to enhance the grip.

The deposit in which *Coelophysis* was discovered was densely packed with skeletons of every stage of growth, from juvenile to adult, most of them completely articulated, so we have a rare glance at a complete cross section of a

---

Saltopus was an early dinosaur embodying most of the features that were to make the subclass Dinosauria so successful. The living animal was about the size of a house cat.

population of this genus. Although no one knows why these animals died together in this manner, the fact that the skeletons remain articulated indicates that they were trapped in some fashion, perhaps by quicksand or some other viscous agency. Perhaps they were a flock that accidentally wandered into whatever trap killed them; then again, some of the smaller animals may have been eaten by larger ones, suggesting that once a few of the animals were trapped, others came looking for easy prey. *Coelophysis* must have been a voracious predator, fast and perpetually hungry, and the sight of any struggling animal may have set off a sequence of attacking so powerful as to have overcome any qualms about either cannibalism or quicksand.

By the Mid- and Upper Jurassic, most coelurosaurs possessed but three fingers, one of which was opposed to the rest for grasping. Giving its name to

Coelophysis, whose skeletons were discovered in a group in New Mexico, was about the mass of a medium-sized dog.

the entire infraorder Coelurosauria is the Upper Jurassic genus *Coelurus,* formerly called *Ornitholestes* ("bird-catcher") because of its agile build. Some two meters long from nose to tip of tail, this animal is portrayed (pages 40–41) with a life-sized drawing of both skull and head to indicate its size.

A smaller coelurosaur, one of the smallest known dinosaurs in fact, was about the size of a crow. Named *Compsognathus longipes*, this central European form was a predator on mammals and insects during Middle and Upper Jurassic times. *Compsognathus* is particularly interesting because a skeleton long supposed to represent this genus was found on closer examination to have

Coelurus was a small dinosaur; restorations of its head and skull are reproduced life-size in the drawings at top. The bottom drawing shows *Coelurus* as a "fossil Lizard," dragging its tail as early paleontologists supposed such animals must.

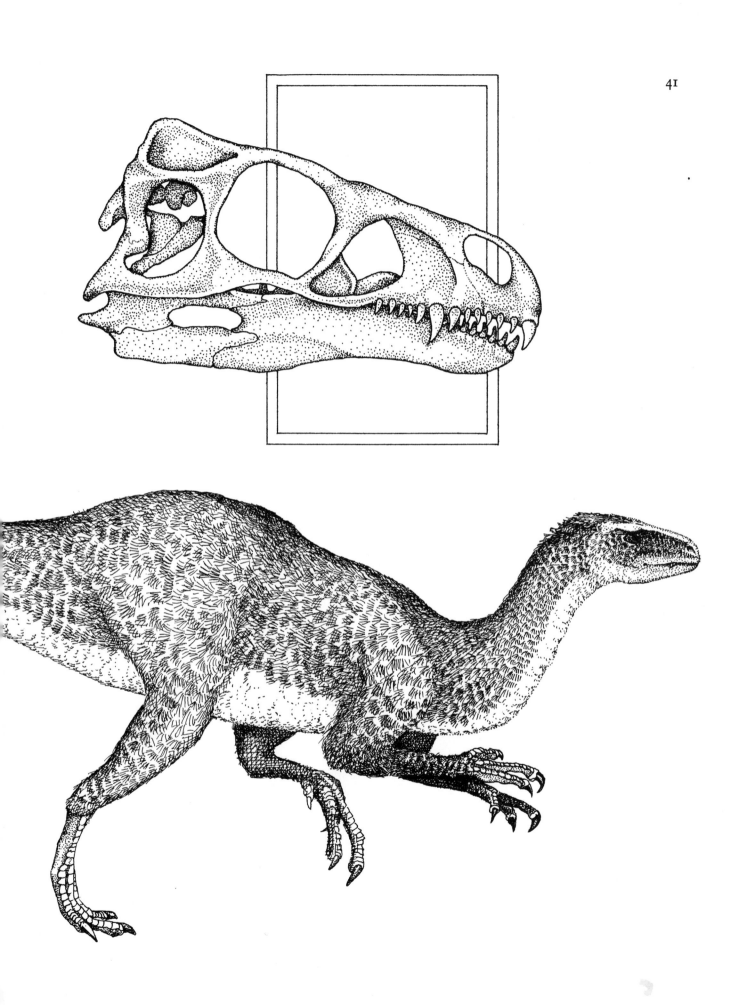

retained some of its feathers and thus, in the usual manner of "fossil Lizard" paleontology, was relegated to the birds!

Actually, the famous aforementioned *Archaeopteryx*, "old wing," long thought to be a transitional bird, was a small coelurosaur so closely related to *Compsognathus* as to be skeletally indistinguishable from it. Indeed, all living birds are built bone for bone on the coelurosaur pattern, on which are superimposed some modifications for flight. In coelurosaurs all the prerequisites for flight—endothermy, feathered insulation, and light build—were present for millions of years before the appearance of the specialized flying dinosaurs we call birds. Luckily, a few of these airy little dinosaurs were caught by gusts of wind and blown into quiet water, where they sank before their feathers deteriorated. *Archaeopteryx* itself, having been so remarkably well preserved, gives a glimpse into the life-style of a little dinosaur predator of the Jurassic. Some of the insulating feathers along its arms and tail had become elongated to provide steering surfaces so that this swift runner could make instant turns and stop on a dime. Not only would this increased agility have facilitated the

---

Archaeopteryx lithographica, with its long feathers, was once supposed to be a bird; however, close examination of its skeleton shows it to be a coelurosaur. Except for their powers of flight, birds may be regarded as little dinosaurs descended from the coelurosaurs.

Saurornithoides may have hunted mammals such as its contemporary the opossum *Didelphis*.

catching of flying insects, but also it would have enabled *Archaeopteryx* (or *Compsognathus*) to avoid larger predators such as *Coelurus* who could not turn nearly so fast in pursuit.

In all, we are forced to conclude that birds are no more or less than dinosaurs, and that their classification outside class Archosauria makes no more sense than would classifying bats outside class Mammalia because they, too, can fly! Thus an observant bird-watcher, immersed in the pursuit of his avocation, may extrapolate from the behavior of birds to catch a glimpse of the mighty Mesozoic in miniature. This point of view, of course, adds considerably to the enchantment of ornithology; more than this, though, it shows that the loveliness of bird life is an echo of an even greater beauty, that of the whole of dinosaur biology of which the birds are the only surviving expressions.

Struthiomimus, the aptly named "ostrich-mimic," was about as large as a man and lived by seeing well and running fast.

During the Cretaceous, the last period of the Mesozoic, the coelurosaurs produced a number of highly specialized forms that were among the brainiest and most astounding of dinosaurs. Best known of these are the ornithomimids, the "bird-mimics," of which *Struthiomimus altus*, the "tall ostrich-mimic," is a familiar example. These creatures must have been among the fastest terrestrial animals ever to have lived. Their small skulls had lost the teeth, replacing them with beaks similar to those of modern birds. The eyes were huge, among the largest known among vertebrates, and must have been extraordinarily acute. The brain was larger than that of the largest modern bird brain, indicating a behavioral repertoire of some complexity, probably involving the complex verbal interactions and flocking characteristic of many modern birds. Ornithomimids were probably omnivorous like ostriches, eating fruits, vegetables, and small vertebrates.

Another Cretaceous coelurosaur, *Saurornithoides*, appears to have been a specialized mammal-catcher. The nocturnal mammals of the time offered a good food source, provided one had very sharp night vision and the ability to outwit the little devils, and the capacity of *Saurornithoides*'s brain and its huge eyes argue strongly in this direction. *Saurornithoides* means "birdlike lizard," an indication of the animal's appearance.

Certain coelurosaurs evolved spectacular tools in the perfection of their hunting techniques. Their descendants include the genus *Dromaeosaurus*, the "emu-lizards," named after the aggressive Australian ground-birds. Dromaeosaurs possessed a highly modified inner hind toe, a sort of built-in switchblade with which these speedy predators literally kicked the stuffing out of prey while holding it with the long "hands." This sort of mayhem, of course, required that the predator stand on one hind leg while kicking with the other, involving a highly developed sense of equilibrium. Dromaeosaur "hands" were equipped with a fully opposable digit like a thumb, and the dromaeosaurs and their relatives had forward-directed, binocular vision and comparatively gigantic brains. Opposable thumb, stereoscopic vision, an enhanced ability to think— such a constellation of attributes offers some interesting room for speculation. What might the coelurosaurs have done if they had not been killed off? What paths might such extraordinary animals have taken in their quest for efficiency? Judging from the appearance of the restoration of the dromaeosaur, I for one am almost pleased that their progress was truncated as it was.

Returning to the early days of the dinosaurs, we come to the second infra-order of suborder Theropoda, infraorder Carnosauria, the "flesh-lizards" of elder paleontology. These originated as close cousins of the coelurosaurs who took to seeking the protein locked up in the large herbivorous dinosaurs of their times. The earliest of these carnivores were the Teratosauridae of the Triassic, of which *Teratosaurus* is the typical genus. Although formerly restored

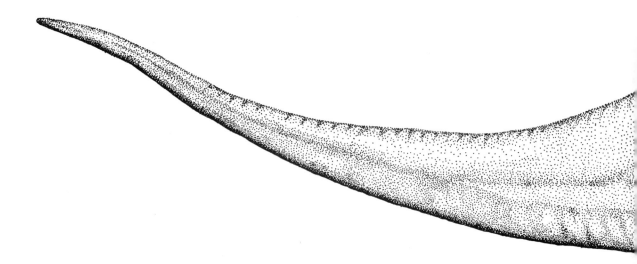

as a reptile with a dragging tail, *Teratosaurus* may be regarded as a great big coelurosaur in structure; where the coelurosaur skeleton was hollow and delicate, the far heavier *Teratosaurus* was correspondingly more massively built, the bones solid and the neck shortened and more powerful to support the large head. However, the basic thecodont pattern remains in the bipedal stance of the animal, its long horizontal tail held stiffly to counterbalance the short body and heavy head, which was armed with curved, serrated, meat-cleaver teeth. The forearms were short and armed with three stout talons for grappling with prey. Teratosaurs were about eight meters long, standing some three meters tall at the head. They were the dominant predators of their times and the prototype for all the more famous carnivores to follow.

During the Jurassic the descendants of teratosaurs produced the family Megalosauridae, named after Dean Buckland's "great fossil Lizard." Far from being the quadrupedal lizards proposed by Buckland, however, the megalo-saurs were gigantic birdlike bipeds of whom the most famous is *Allosaurus,*

Dromaeosaurus was a fearsome-looking man-sized predator that kicked its prey apart with a modified inner toe.

the "weird lizard," originally dubbed the "leaping lizard" because its American discoverer assumed from its long hind legs that it was a kangaroolike reptile that *bounced* on its prey. Actually, *Allosaurus* was a walker and a runner and must have been very fast indeed with a three-meter stride at the trot.

Evidence in fossil tracks showing allosaurs following large herbivores, plus unmistakable tooth marks on the bones of its gigantic plant-eating contemporaries, suggest that *Allosaurus* was accustomed to killing and eating animals far larger than itself. Because predators that work alone, such as mountain lions, tend to kill prey their own size or smaller, the implication is that megalosaurs, like humans and wolves, killed such large prey by hunting in

Teratosaurus was a primitive Triassic carnosaur that may have weighed a ton or more.

organized groups or at least pairs. Indeed, there is every reason to suppose that these animals followed herds of sauropod dinosaurs much as wolves follow caribou, weeding out the old, the infirm, and the unprotected young, and that the symbiotic sauropod-megalosaur relationships paralleled in every way those of mammals in similar ecologic niches. The sight of a pack of allosaurs striding tall and graceful across the Mesozoic savannah must have been among the most beautiful and awesome offered by the living system in any age.

In the Cretaceous, the ecologic niche occupied by large predators passed from the megalosaurs to their more specialized descendants the *Tyrannosauridae*, "tyrant-lizards," of which *Tyrannosaurus rex* is the best known. Traditionally typecast as a B-movie heavy, *Tyrannosaurus* is pictured as a lumbering tripod whose long, flexible tail dragged behind him as he moved, painfully slowly, toward a nubile maiden or other delicacy. In fact, *Tyrannosaurus* shared with his relatives the stiffened tail that never touched the ground when the animal

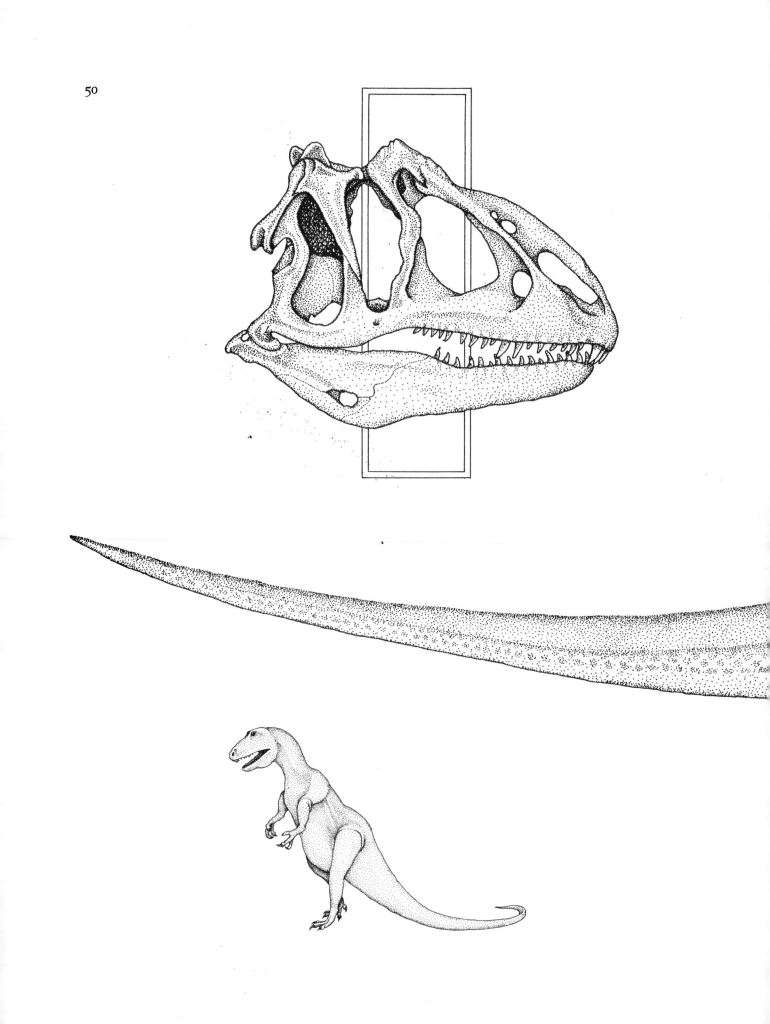

was walking. He was a biped rather than a tripod; he came equipped with a long and rapid stride that enabled him to catch the swift herbivores that were his food while circumventing their fearsome spines, horns, and other defenses. The front feet in tyrannosaurids were more reduced than those of their ancestors, possessing only two fingers and being too short even to reach the mouth.

This development occurred in response to the prey with which these animals were forced to contend, prey of a more prickly and ferocious nature by far than the gentle sauropods pursued by megalosaurs. Grappling a horned

---

Allosaurus fragilis and its skull. The small drawing shows this American megalosaur as a "great fossil Lizard," in the familiar tripodal stance with dragging tail. Compare this drawing with the old British restoration on p. 7.

ceratopsian dinosaur with the forelimbs could be fatal for a predatory dinosaur, and the tyrannosaurs surmounted this problem by towering over such prey and attacking from above with the fearsomely armed mouth. The forelimbs had become mere hooks to stabilize the animal when he raised his several tons off the ground after a rest. Extending his hind legs, a tyrannosaur would simply slide backward were there not something—the claws of his forefeet—to prevent this sliding by hooking into the earth.

Other tyrannosaurids, such as *Gorgosaurus*, were somewhat smaller but similar in general plan to *Tyrannosaurus*. They share the highly specialized predatory form that led some early paleontologists to speculate that such animals were actually scavengers: No mere lizard could have captured active prey if he had such mass to lug around with him, and the tyrannosaurs lacked the powerful forelimbs with which their ancestors manipulated prey. However, we now understand that these were far from lizards; every detail of the tyrannosaur frame argues for an active predatory life-style.

Tyrannosaurids brings the evolutionary story of the carnosaurs to its culmination. Possessing perhaps the largest brains of any dinosaurs, they appear to have hunted in delicately organized packs after the manner of their megalosaurian ancestors, a strategy that was necessary for attacking the most powerful and best-defended herbivores the earth has ever seen. Tyrannosaurid eyes were sharp and protected from glare by a supraorbital ridge like that in eagles. Also like eagles, tyrannosaurids possessed mighty talons on their four hind toes with which they impaled their prey while tearing at it with their teeth. In a way, these great beasts were among the most birdlike of their terrestrial relatives, for the reduced front limbs, like those of birds, had lost their grasping function completely. This resemblance to birds, however, only serves to increase the fearsome aspect of these mightiest of all land-dwelling predators; one can imagine circumventing somehow a hulking tripodal lizard, but the bright-eyed, five-meter-tall, eaglelike tyrannosaur of modern paleontology, hunting his prey in packs, would present quite a problem, even to the handsomest and most machismo-rich movie hero.

Between the Carnosauria and Coelurosauria, the predatory niches available to dinosaurs were so completely filled that suborder Theropoda contains all the predators produced during the Mesozoic by dinosaurs. The obvious efficiency of these varied hunters leads us to some interesting conclusions about their behavior, conclusions which may seem unpalatable to "great fossil Lizard" advocates, but which are nonetheless almost unavoidable in light of the evidence presented here. Besides, this sort of speculation is always a lot of fun.

For instance, an endothermic predator goes through a great deal of energy in conducting his affairs; as we have seen, he requires a large number of herbivores, and therefore space, to support him. Land inhabited by such energy-intensive animals tends to be divided up among them, theoretically spacing them so that each individual and group enjoys stability through adequate resources. In fact, changes in population and environment constantly alter the amount of available resources, and territorial conflict is inevitable. All this is as true of archosaurs as it is of wolves and men.

Since all of the carnivorous dinosaurs were lethally armed, it is likely that complicated rituals of aggression and appeasement evolved to reduce the chances for actual bodily injury in territorial disputes. We are thus led to imagine many a spectacular boundary-line dance between rival landholders, with flash-patterns and other bodily markings as well as all manner of loud noises serving to delineate territories. Again, we turn to birds, coelurosaur descendants, for a glimpse at what these territorial discussions were like—and, as we all know, the territorial displays of birds involve some of the most swashbuckling behavior in the animal kingdom.

Young dinosaurs must have been nearly helpless or at best highly vulnerable to all their hungry sharp-eyed cousins. Since parental care is highly developed in both living archosaur groups, the primitive crocodilians and the advanced birds, one is inclined to suspect the same of their extinct relatives. It is likely that many young dinosaurs were protected in crèches, nesting areas guarded by their parents, until the young were large enough to move with the group or set off on their own. Obviously, a newly hatched dinosaur twenty centimeters long would be hard put to keep up with its six-meter parent, or keep from being trodden on! The fact that fossils of very young dinosaurs are rarely found seems to support this point, arguing that young were carefully protected rather than abandoned to their fates.

Of course, all these ravenous predators were supported by a vast collection of herbivores, one group of which had its origin in suborder Theropoda. Infra-order Prosauropoda was a group of primitive Triassic genera that showed divergence from the original biped-carnivore plan toward one specialized in vegetarianism and a return to quadrupedal locomotion. Prosauropoda means "before the lizard-feet," indicating the transitional position of these animals between early carnivorous forms and the immense herbivorous, long-necked, long-tailed sauropods that almost instantly come to mind when we think of dinosaurs.

Typical of the Prosauropoda was the Upper Triassic European *Plateosaurus,* the "flat lizard." *Plateosaurus* was far from flat, being rather corpulent and,

Tyrannosaurus rex, the largest known terrestrial predator, killed with his hind talons and serrate teeth. A grown man's head would be level with the knee of this tiger of the Mesozoic. The small drawing shows the classic "great fossil Lizard" representation of the tyrannosaurs.

when standing bipedally erect, as much as five meters tall. Its skull is generally similar to that of the coelurosaurs, but blunter and fitted with many closely spaced triangular teeth more adapted to manipulation of vegetation than holding struggling prey. However, these teeth are still pointed, and *Plateosaurus* may have been an omnivore, occasionally plucking up some small animal to vary its diet.

The small head of *Plateosaurus* seems ridiculously out of proportion to its bulky torso and legs, a condition carried to extremes in its sauropod descendants. This seemingly malproportioned build reflects digestive adjustments involved in the change from carnivory to herbivory. The carnivorous ancestors of *Plateosaurus* had short digestive tracts like most carnivorous animals, for meat requires less work before it can be used by the body. On the other hand, land vegetation is composed largely of cellulose, a compound indigestible to most animals. Cellulose, the woody matter of plants, not only is the most abundant substance (except water) by mass in terrestrial vegetation, but is also an energy-rich carbohydrate in which is stored much of the sun's warmth. Therefore the advantage to any animal able to assimilate cellulose is considerable.

Now, while cellulose is not digestible to many animals, it is both highly digestible to and relished by certain bacteria and protozoa. In many instances throughout land vertebrate history, herbivores have circumvented the cellulose problem by enlisting the aid of such microorganisms in digestion. This is accomplished when an herbivore provides said microorganisms with fermentation chambers somewhere along its digestive tract in which they may digest vast quantities of cellulose in a warm, moist, peaceful environment. When the fermentation is finished, the mass of microorganisms and digested plant matter

Gorgosaurus, a "small" (3.5 meters tall) tyrannosaurid from the Upper Cretaceous of North America. Adult gorgosaurs probably weighed a ton or so, but could move extremely speedily in pursuit of prey.

is assimilated as food by the herbivore possessing this elegant digestive tract, and the process is begun again.

This herbivore-microorganism symbiosis is employed by many herbivores among the higher animals. Mammalian ruminants such as cattle and deer are famous for their extra "stomachs," in which this fermentation takes place, but other herbivorous mammals carry out the same process—horses and their relatives in a pocket of the large intestine, rabbits in a two-stage eating process where their feces are run through again for good measure. Kangaroos, the largest grazers of the Australian marsupial fauna, have evolved analogous

---

Plateosaurus and its skull. These prosauropods, while still capable of running on their hind legs, were down on all fours much of the time.

digestive pockets along the stomach, and among the invertebrates, the lowly cockroaches have done the same.

Naturally, to be effectively fermented inside an herbivore, such fibrous plant matter must be ground up. This is accomplished in mammals by grinding teeth, the molars, but no archosaur possesses grinding teeth. Instead, these animals rely on their gizzards, muscular mills adjacent to the stomach and lined with hard plates and sandpaperlike surfaces. Archosaurs, from crocodiles to birds, swallow stones to enhance the grinding action in their gizzards, so no archosaur skull ever need be weighted down with the heavy molars present in most herbivorous mammals. Thus the head remains light and mobile on its long neck, while the mass of gizzardstones remains nearer the center of gravity to enhance balance. Furthermore, archosaurs are able to take big bites and swallow quickly without chewing, as the chewing is done internally. Gastroliths, or "bellystones," are those rocks swallowed by dinosaurs that became too smooth to be effective in grinding and were discarded and replaced. Such stones are found by the thousands in some dinosaur-bearing strata.

Anyway, because of the fibrous nature of cellulose-containing food, the prosauropod gizzard was probably correspondingly large and powerful. The fermentation chambers added further bulk to the digestive system, and this increase in mass is reflected in the heavy build and semiquadrupedal gait of prosauropods. The rib cage is broadened considerably to make room for the new equipment, while the hind legs are adapted to carry great weight. The tail is deepened to provide mass offsetting the mass of the body's forepart in bipedal walking; when sitting around eating or digesting, as all large herbivores must at times, the animal remained on all fours to conserve energy.

The prosauropod's tendency to drop onto all fours when moving slowly caused the forelegs to become correspondingly larger and more massive as they supported more and more digestive equipment. The primitive, five-fingered forefeet are fitted with an enlarged, hooked first-finger claw, perhaps useful in rooting and grubbing, or in pulling branches to the mouth, and probably serving as this inoffensive form's only active defense other than running away. The other four fingers are tipped with short, blunt, hooflike nails on which the animal could comfortably walk. When alarmed, however, prosauropods could quickly assume a bipedal stride for a sprint to safety.

The small head of the prosauropod spent most of its time stoking the

---

Diplodocus, a grazer of tall trees, may have wrapped its whiplash tail around the trunk of a nearby tree to steady itself on its hind legs. When walking, *Diplodocus* used all fours like the rest of the Sauropoda, a dinosaur group that secondarily returned to quadrupedal locomotion.

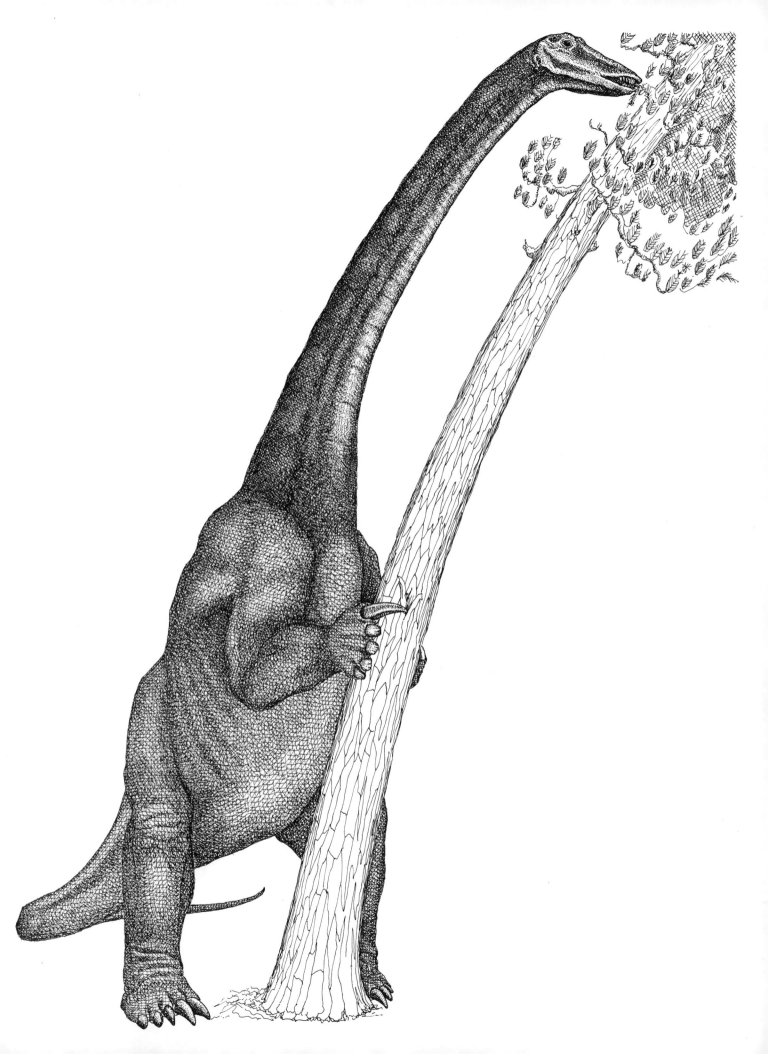

tremendous fermentation chambers below. The long neck permitted both grazing of short plants close to the ground and plucking fronds from tall ones, for these animals stood several meters high when they wished. Vegetation was abundant, for these were the first animals to exploit the large-endotherm browser niche; they had no competition, and at least at first, the plants had no defense against this new onslaught. Of course this situation changed—shorter plants responded by becoming too tough or thorny for the simple teeth of prosauropods, while tall plants grew taller.

It was the quest for the foliage of taller and taller trees, especially conifers, that was responsible for the unique specializations of suborder Sauropoda. These astonishing animals, among whom are the largest land animals known, personify the dinosaurs for millions of people through such familiar symbols as the Sinclair Oil Corporation dinosaur. With their long necks and tails, small heads, and immense legs, they represent the logical outcome of the prosauropods' race with the trees for height.

The general picture of sauropods as browsers from the branches of tall conifer trees is borne out by the explosion of such trees across the early Jurassic landscape, simultaneous with that of the sauropods. The energy stored in the foliage of tall conifer trees had been untapped by vertebrate animals before the advent of the sauropods, so that much of the planet's biomass rested in this foliage. The prosauropods seem to have been the first vertebrates to develop sufficient height and the proper digestive processes to break into this lucrative niche. Their success at this game was so great that their descendants, the sauropods, evolved a number of genera in different parts of the world, based on the same general plan but varying according to the trees each preferred.

Best known of these are probably the North American "thunder lizards," the brontosaurs, heavyset forms with spatulate (spoon-shaped) teeth for eating coarser leaves. Their cousins in genus *Diplodocus* were far longer, lighter, positively attenuated forms that must have specialized in the very tops of trees; these were the longest animals ever to have walked the earth, being perhaps twenty-five meters in length. Diplodocids possessed peglike teeth that are usually heavily worn in front from perpetually stripping woody branches of their foliage. The skeleton shows that *Diplodocus* may have been able to rise on its hind legs with little difficulty, to reach the lovely new tender shoots at the tips of tall trees and to defend itself against predators by swinging the great hooked claws on the first fingers of each forefoot. *Diplodocus* means

---

Brachiosaurus, the "arm lizard," largest of land animals.

The first people to discover the bones of sauropods supposed them to be the remains of marine "whale-lizards," and invested these animals with a vertical fluke on the tail (*top*). When careful examination definitely showed these animals to be land dwellers, "great fossil Lizard" proponents postulated a crawling stance (*middle*). However, sauropod bones actually articulate in a definitely vertical stance, and the "fossil Lizard" people eventually relegated these mighty animals to lakes and swamps, where they were said to snorkel about with their long necks and to dine on "soft aquatic vegetation."

"double-beamed," referring to the mighty supporting structures in the animal's spine.

Yet another group of sauropods, the brachiosaurs ("arm lizards"), gave up rising on their hind legs but continued to insist, like diplodocids, on the very tops of trees. In a condition rare in dinosaurs, *Brachiosaurus* and its close relatives possessed forelegs markedly longer than their hind legs. Standing four stories tall on all fours, *Brachiosaurus* was able to consume more vegetation than its cousins because its giant forelegs supported far more mass in digestive equipment than could be carried by other sauropods. *Brachiosaurus* approached the theoretical limits to size in land animals; some isolated bones may represent individuals weighing ninety tons, as much as a large whale.

The huge size of sauropod bones prompted their earliest discoverers to label them cetiosaurs ("whale-lizards"), and it was proposed that they were marine animals propelled by webbed feet and a finned tail. By the time the first entire skeletons of sauropods had been discovered, in the mid-nineteenth century, it became evident that these were *walking* animals with straight, pillarlike legs like those of elephants.

Although this discovery forced the sauropods out of the oceans, the natural conservatism of science kept them in the water—this time in swamps and lakes, where they were said to have spent their lives floating about eating "soft aquatic vegetation" with their little teeth. It was said that the long neck enabled the animals to snorkel air from the water's surface while sitting safe on the bottom. In addition, the sauropod nostrils are often located high on the head; it was suggested that such placement of the nostrils permitted the animals to hide in water with only their nostrils protruding.

Sauropods suffered further indignity from paleontologists when it was suggested that they might have crawled with their bellies on the ground like the great fossil lizards they were supposed to be. This amusing idea was quickly dispelled by close examination of the bones, which clearly show a straight-legged, fully erect posture. The swamp-and-lake-dweller hypothesis lived on, however, especially in light of the (correct!) assumption that no great fossil lizard could weigh so much and get around without some external means of support.

Problems have always plagued the swamp-dweller model of the sauropods. For instance, the entire sauropod skeleton is built with a strong emphasis on lightness. However, in air-breathing animals such as whales and hippopotamuses, the skeletal emphasis is on *increase* in mass; otherwise, having taken a good breath to submerge, such animals would continue to float unless they expended a great deal of precious oxygen attempting to stay beneath the surface. The remains of sauropods also suggest that these animals were equipped with an extensive system of air sacs, aiding them in cooling and considerably reducing their masses. Such creatures would have floated like corks in the water.

Again, it is probable that the mechanics of resting on a lake bottom six meters below the water's surface and breathing through a long neck are beyond the capability of the systems represented by sauropod bones. Such breathing would have to displace several hundred kilograms of water, an unlikely feat for any sauropod. And if sauropods spent so much of their time "hiding" in the water, from what were they hiding? Certainly not from the prodigious crocodilians of their time, any one of which could easily have drowned a sauropod by clinging to its neck. These efficient predators dominated the swamps of the Mesozoic and surely made life miserable for any large vertebrates that crossed their paths.

Finally there is the problem of what food might have been available to support swamp-dwelling sauropods. Their simple spoon- or peg-shaped teeth seem unsuited to any known form of aquatic vegetation (although admirably suited to stripping foliage from trees), and some impressive stretches of the imagination are required to feed aquatic sauropods. For instance, in addition to the "soft aquatic vegetation" hypothesis, there is a theory that sauropods were mollusk eaters, plucking clams and mussels from the mud of the shores. Some people have suggested that they were scavengers, feeding on each other's carcasses, but this is an ecologic situation similar to the economic one of the town where all the citizens are mechanics repairing each other's cars. Whatever it was that they ate, it wore the teeth of most sauropods considerably; it was probably vegetation, but it certainly was not soft.

As we have seen, the swamp-dwelling sauropod is passing the way of all great fossil lizard models and is in the process of being replaced by a picture of the upland sauropod browsing on the foliage of conifers and other tall trees. With each meter in height gained by the dominant conifer trees of the time, the sauropods followed suit. Each meter gained by the dinosaurs taxed their huge fermenting digestive systems more heavily, resulting in proportionally greater mass. They lost their bipedal walk forever, their forelegs becoming mighty supports for the neck, the main organ for height. The rear legs, under the weight of many tons, became columns as vertical as those in a Greek temple. Together with the pelvis and the strikingly tall sacral vertebrae, these legs formed a tower from which the rest of the spinal column was suspended in the exact manner of a suspension bridge. The stiff tail of the bipedal ancestors continued stiff, its rigidity enhanced by the fusing of some of its vertebrae; since this huge tail was probably held in the air as the sauropod walked, the familiar old tail-dragging great fossil lizard restorations are probably as out-dated as the swamp-dweller models. In some species this tail could be lifted high in the air in conjunction with the lifting of the front part of the body, by contraction of the muscles originating in the spines of the tall sacral vertebrae; thus these gigantic animals could tower on their hind legs to reach the higher branches.

Because the process of eating was almost perpetual in such energy-consumptive gargantuans, the head was in constant motion as it stripped the nutritious needles from branches and sent them down the long neck-chute to the digestive factory below. While in large sauropods this head was at least as large as that of

Some of the engineering triumphs of the Sauropoda, including the hollowed-out, weight-saving vertebrae and suspension-bridge pelvic girdle, are shown in this drawing. The skull of *Camarasaurus* shows the large nostril (N) and the light build of the head of sauropods.

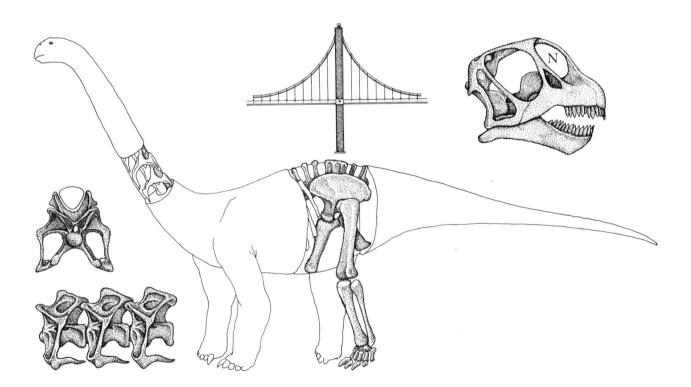

a cow, it was actually smaller in diameter than some of the neck vertebrae. This comparatively tiny head, long an object of ridicule among critics of the sauropods, was necessary because of its great height above the ground; not only must its weight be kept as small as possible, but the animal's mighty heart had its limits and could not have pumped enough blood to nourish a bigger head so high far away. In all sauropods the skull is a light, airy structure equipped with peglike teeth admirably designed for their task of stripping foliage. This skull contained a brain about the size of that of a dog, in some large sauropods equivalent to but a few hundred-thousandths of the total body mass.

Because its head was so small in relation to the rest of the sauropod, the stoking process had to be accelerated in order to pass enough food through this narrow portal. This was accomplished with the evolution of nostrils placed high on the skull, so that the animals might eat constantly without having this all-important task interfere with the breathing process. In addition, these nostrils opened onto an enlarged nasal chamber, permitting an acute sense of smell with which the sauropods might locate food and predators.

The sauropod neck was a living crane for lifting the head to food; in keeping with this function it was designed with lightness as the prime consideration. The twelve to fifteen sauropod neck vertebrae provided strength and flexibility to a neck up to seven meters long. A U-shaped bracket in the top of each of these beautiful vertebrae served as a guide for a stout cablelike ligament that ran the length of the neck and was responsible for lifting the head high in the air. The articulations between the neck vertebrae are unique among backboned animals in possessing extra articulations to combine strength with agility, while the vertebrae themselves are elegantly hollowed out to minimize their masses.

Their skeletons show in sauropods an intention to move on land, and move fast at that. Their tracks indicate that they moved in herds across the Mesozoic landscape, literally designing with their immense appetites the great conifers that supported them. It has been suggested that sauropod young were born alive and able to move with the herd and enjoy its protection from birth; certainly the absence of young sauropod remains suggests a degree of parental protection, and a herd of such behemoths would be almost immune to predation.

Sauropods survived through more than a hundred million years of changing times, sticking with their great food-trees through thick and thin until the collapse of their ecologic world at the end of the Mesozoic; then, with all the other terrestrial dinosaurs, they disappeared.

But the trees remain. To walk among Ponderosa pines, Douglas firs, or

sequoias is to walk in the Mesozoic when these stately plants covered much of
the earth. Unlike the dinosaurs, the trees survived the end of their era and
continue growing fast and tall, to the delight of foresters and home builders.
They offer us a memory of the sauropods who walked among them in the
time of their making, the long-gone sauropods whose majestic height is still
reflected in the grandeur of the big trees.

Standing in a conifer forest, we can envision the progress of a herd of
sauropods among the trees, necks weaving gracefully through the dappled
green, perhaps a little pack of megalosaurs moving watchfully alongside. Who
knows? Perhaps amid the roar and crash of logging operations, the old forests
recall the company of their vanished coevolvers; the rich, warm piny breath
and gentle stupid eyes of the sauropods seem so much more elegantly suited
to these cathedral woods than the bully-whiskered presence of the woodsman,
the screaming violence of his saw.

ORNITHISCHIA

So far we have traced the histories of the carnivorous dinosaurs and of some of the herbivores on which they fed. However, the sauropods, lovers of conifers, were specialized to such trees, while other forms of vegetation continued for a time unmolested by large land vertebrates. It remained for another group to exploit the energy of the great majority of Mesozoic plant species, including the palmlike cycads, the broad-leaved ginkgoes, and later, the flowering plants whose descendants dominate the land flora today.

The digestive problems confronting any potential conqueror of this opulent niche were similar to those posed to the prosauropods in their conversion from flesh-eating to plant-eating, mainly involving the evolution of a system capable of processing enough cellulose-rich plants to continue energizing a large endothermic metabolic system. However, the plants available after the success of the sauropods were, as we have seen, those that were hard, thorny, or extremely fibrous, requiring the eater to have special equipment just to get them into his mouth. Such well-defended plants continued unmolested for a time, until at some point during the Upper Triassic a dinosaur appeared that was capable of penetrating these defenses.

Although the earliest fossils of these coarse-plant eaters are rare and inadequately publicized, we find a good representative of their basic form in the later Jurassic genus *Hypsilophodon*, an animal whose name refers to the specialized coarse-plant *shearing* (rather than plucking, as in sauropods) teeth. With these improved teeth dinosaurs were able to mush up all manner of otherwise unpalatable plants; in addition, the evolution of a hooked horn beak replacing the ancestral foreteeth enabled the animal to take an efficient bite out of the hardest of plant substances. *Hypsilophodon* thus removed pieces of plants with its beak, chopped them into swallowable form with its shearing hind teeth, and then ran them through a massive digestive system run on the familiar fermentation principle.

In *Hypsilophodon* and its relatives there is evidence that the huge fermentation pots of the digestive system were located in the lower end of the digestive tract, for in these animals the pelvis has been significantly altered from the old triradiate thecodont pattern to produce a great deal of space in the lower abdomen. More specifically, the forward-leaning pubic bone of the thecodont ancestor has been rotated backward to lie along the ischium, although a projection of the pubis remains along each side of the animal's body to support the massive intestines and serve as a point of origin for the powerful hind leg muscles. In this way the greatest digestive mass was hung beneath the center of gravity at the hip, reducing the need to return to quadrupedalism, as did the prosauropods, and permitting *Hypsilophodon* and most of its descendants to remain efficient bipeds. Because this new hip arrangement is said to resemble that of modern birds, the entire order of animals possessing it is named the Ornithischia, "bird-hips," to distinguish them from their "lizard-hipped" cousins, the Saurischia.

Like their cousins, the original Ornithischia were fast, light bipeds. *Hypsilophodon* reflects this pattern in its long hind legs and feet, designed to propel the animal to safety in a rapid bounding run. Although some old restorations show *Hypsilophodon* sitting in trees with a prehensile tail wrapped around a branch, the animal was actually equipped with the usual stiff archosaur appendage and, at about two meters in length, seems to have been the ecologic equivalent of a small deer, antelope, or goat.

This parallel is further enhanced by the beak and shearing teeth, an arrangement remarkably similar in some respects to that found in ruminant mammals. Instead of the beak, such mammals possess sharp incisor teeth in the forepart of the lower jaw, which operate against a toothless horny pad in the upper. This biting tool is backed up by a toothless space and then a battery of grinding teeth, for mammals have no gizzards. In ornithischia the jaws and their muscles are so designed that highly fibrous plant matter may be reduced in an up-and-down, fore-and-aft motion, while in ruminants the motion is side to side. Ornithischians further parallel ruminants in the evolution of strong cheek muscles along the outsides of the jaws.

From some Upper Triassic *Hypsilophodon*-like ancestor the Ornithischia quickly radiated into nearly every ecologic niche available to large endothermic herbivores able to handle tough plant matter. Because there was no competition for these many niches, the Ornithischia early showed a tendency toward larger

Hypsilophodon, a primitive ornithischian illustrating some of the adaptations responsible for the immense success of its order. The small drawings below show the location of the digestive organs in dinosaurs. The primitive dinosaur (*top*) was a bipedal carnivore with a relatively small digestive system resting on the pubic bone, in front of the center of gravity at the hip joint. Sauropods (*center*) managed the increase in size of the vegetarian digestive system by dropping onto all fours, distributing the weight of digestive organs to the forefeet. Ornithischians (*bottom*) maintained the biped stance by moving the pubic bone of the hip backward, centering the digestive mass beneath the center of gravity. In the diagrams of dinosaur hips (*right*) the pubic bone is shaded; in saurischians it is pointed forward, in ornithischians compressed back with the movement of the digestive mass. *Opposite*: The skull of *Hypsilophodon*, showing the cropping "beak" and shearing cheek teeth of ornithischians (*far left*), and their parallels with dentition of modern grazing and browsing mammals such as the American pronghorn (*upper left*). *Lower left*: The massive cheek muscles with which the food mass was held in the mouth. These muscles are omitted in most restorations, giving ornithischian dinosaurs an improperly "lizardlike" look, popular in bygone times.

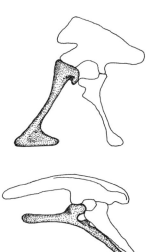

size. The ability to consume plants of all sizes permitted ornithischians to stretch for tree-limb browsing or drop onto their forelegs for a nibble close to the ground. This option is visible in the Mid-Jurassic genus *Camptosaurus*, which contained a number of species of small and medium size. The camptosaur forefeet are heavier by far than those in *Hypsilophodon*, implying that, although camptosaurs were capable of fast bipedal locomotion in a hurry, they spent a good deal of time consuming some sort of ground-level vegetation. The largest camptosaurs were about five meters long.

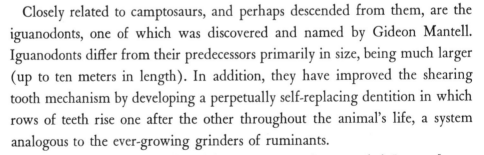

Closely related to camptosaurs, and perhaps descended from them, are the iguanodonts, one of which was discovered and named by Gideon Mantell. Iguanodonts differ from their predecessors primarily in size, being much larger (up to ten meters in length). In addition, they have improved the shearing tooth mechanism by developing a perpetually self-replacing dentition in which rows of teeth rise one after the other throughout the animal's life, a system analogous to the ever-growing grinders of ruminants.

As we have seen, Mantell and his contemporaries regarded *Iguanodon* as a giant lizard that stumbled about on all fours; discovery of a cone-shaped bone among the remains led these Britishers to endow the animal with a horn on its nose like that of a rhinoceros! When more complete finds became available

Camptosaurus browsing on a cycad, one of the dominant plants of the Jurassic and a thorny, tough plant on which ornithischians probably throve.

and the bipedal stance of *Iguanodon* was confirmed, the cone was found to be a spike mounted on the animal's thumb, the only defensive equipment possessed by these gentle beasts.

An interesting find of a host of *Iguanodon* skeletons in a Belgian coal mine suggests that the animals constituted a herd that was frightened into a crevasse by the approach of predators. All of these skeletons are adult, indicating that the iguanodonts may have raised their young in crèches, perhaps feeding them with regurgitated food in the manner of some birds and mammals today.

From some form closely related to the iguanodonts arose the famous "duck-billed" dinosaurs of the Cretaceous period. These successful animals compose the family Hadrosauridae, named after the typical genus, the Upper Cretaceous *Hadrosaurus* ("big lizard"). The first complete dinosaur excavated in North

---

Iguanodon possessed defensive spines on its thumbs, with which it must have struck at the eyes of carnivores—there was no other spot at which predatory dinosaurs would be vulnerable to these little weapons.

America, *Hadrosaurus* was discovered in a New Jersey quarry in 1858. Its discoverer recognized that the remains were closely related to Mantell's *Iguanodon*, then still regarded as a quadrupedal great fossil lizard. However, the skeleton of *Hadrosaurus* showed that this animal possessed hind legs that were far longer than the forelegs, sadly confusing the infant world of paleontology, which was as yet unacquainted with the bipedal nature of most dinosaurs. Confronted with the disparity in leg length, some people suggested that *Hadrosaurus* hopped like a kangaroo and, when standing still, balanced on hind legs and tail while browsing on leaves. But since no great fossil lizard could have stood up in this manner, the discoverer of *Hadrosaurus* was forced to conclude that the animal lay on its belly and hopped like a gigantic frog!

Even after they established that *Hadrosaurus* was indeed a biped, early paleontologists continued to malign the animal in their attempts at restoration. It is entertaining in retrospect to follow the logic of the great fossil lizard proponents; extrapolating from the animal's beak, rather wider than that of *Iguanodon* and dubbed a "duckbill," they attributed to *Hadrosaurus* a diet and life-style similar to those of modern ducks! This in spite of the fact that *Hadrosaurus* outweighed the modern duck by many thousands of pounds and possessed literally thousands of hard, sharp teeth, in contrast to the toothless mouth of the duck. Restorations of hadrosaurs still often neglect the powerful cheek muscles, leaving long "lips" to the hinge of the jaws and increasing the animals' resemblance to modern ducks.

Relegated to dabbling about the shores of bodies of water like modern ducks, hadrosaurs were assumed to be capital swimmers; therefore the highly visible stiffening trusses along the tail were ignored, and this appendage was assumed to be a flexible scull with which the animal propelled itself through the water. The general image of the hadrosaurs was one of amphibious living, with the animals coming ashore to crop foliage occasionally but retreating to the water when predators appeared.

Some hadrosaurs have been preserved as "mummies," having died, become dried out, and then been either covered with windblown sand or washed to some quiet body of water where they were buried before the remaining skin and flesh could deteriorate further. The fact that several hadrosaurs have been found in this condition indicates that these animals tended to keep to dry uplands, where their corpses were often subjected to dessication. Furthermore, close examination of the petrified stomach contents of these stony mummies has revealed traces of their last meals. In every case so far studied, the animals had eaten coarse upland plants, leaves, twigs, and the like, rather than the sort of swamp vegetation that ducks might enjoy.

Unfortunately for the "duckbill" model, all evidence suggests that the hadrosaurs were upland browsers and grazers on silica-rich fibrous plant matter, rather in the fashion of modern antelope. Also like antelope, these animals developed a speed and grace rarely to be equaled among land dwellers—particularly those of several tons' mass. Although for grazing on low vegetation the hadrosaurs could walk well enough on four feet, when slipping into

The hadrosaur *Parasaurolophus* in a dry upland climate, in which it appears rather more at home than in steaming swamps and the like. Other hadrosaurs shared with this genus the alternative quadruped-biped stance; in general these animals appear to have occupied the econiches in which we find deer and antelope today. Although most of them weighed several tons, hadrosaurs were obviously built to outrun the great predators of their time.

high gear they ran bipedally. The adaptations for speed in hadrosaur hind legs parallel those in speedy herbivorous mammals. The feet were equipped with hooves for maximum bite into the ground, while the muscle structure cushioned the powerful blows of the feet against the earth and sprang the animal on its way.

Hadrosaurus and its close relatives were rather flat-headed beings, their long noses blending smoothly into the tops of their heads. However, some of the hadrosaurs have become justly famous for their crests, bony excrescences on the tops of their heads which in some cases contain extensions of the nasal cavities. While some hadrosaurs never made it to the hollow-crest stage, contenting themselves with thickenings and extensions of the nasal bones, in others the crests sometimes reached large size, often extending far beyond the skull

itself. Those hadrosaurs with hollow crests exhibit a bewildering array of forms, from genera possessing relatively subdued hollow bulges along the top of the skull to some equipped with nasal bones amazingly expanded into long hollow tubes, helmets, and other protuberances.

Ever since the discovery of hollow-crested hadrosaurs, speculation has been rife as to the possible functions of the crests. Because the animals were supposed to have been water dwellers, many paleontologists suggested that the nasal tubes within the crests were somehow related to breathing while submerged. For example, in forms where the nasal passages looped up over the back of the skull, perhaps air trapped within the crest served as a valve to prevent water from entering the lungs; however, experiments have since shown that water pressure would have pushed that trapped air right on into the animals' lungs, and water would have followed.

Some workers thought that the hollows within the crests stored air while the animals were submerged; but the volume of the space within the crest was so much smaller than the animals' lung capacities as to render this hypothesis silly. One eccentric suggested that this ornamentation was sexual, rather like the plumage of male birds or the manes of lions; but the flat-headed "females" and crested "males" occurred in different areas and time spans, a strong argument against any possibility of success in such animals!

Finally, it has been suggested that the enlarged nasal space permitted by the hollow crests served to increase the area of the epithelial lining of the hadrosaur's nose, allowing a greatly enhanced sense of smell. In mammals the turbinals, thin sheets of curved bone within the nasal cavities, perform this same function within a relatively small volume; the archosaurs, possessing no turbinals, were forced to enlarge the volume of the nasal cavity itself to achieve the same effect.

This last proposition is the best available to us at present. For peaceful animals like the hadrosaurs, an improved sense of smell must have been essential to warn of the approach of carnosaurs, and the great success and diversity of hollow-crested hadrosaurs indicates that the improvement was valid.

There remains the problem of the great variety of crest shapes and sizes sported by the hadrosaurs. Certainly, in the random fashion by which natural selection works, there is room for many differences; attention is often called to the various closely related species of African antelope whose horns are all markedly different in shape, although all perform the same functions. It may be that the different crests served simply as marks of recognition within a species; if the hadrosaurs of different species herded together, as seems likely,

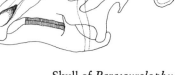

Skull of *Parasaurolophus cyrtocristatus,* showing path of nasal cavity (dotted line).

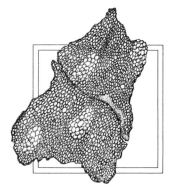

A portion of fossilized skin from *Anatosaurus,* showing a leathery texture similar to that of large modern mammals.

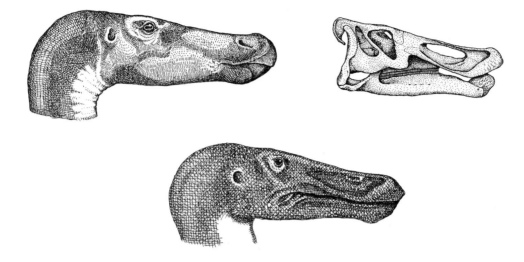

Top: Head and skull restoration of *Anatosaurus,* a typical crestless hadrosaur. *Above center*: Restoration of the head as "great fossil Lizard," with duckbill formed by omission of cheek muscles and sensitive nasal cavity.

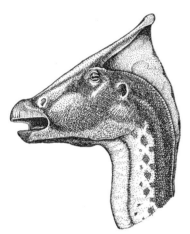

Saurolophus angustirostris

Cheneosaurus tolmanensis

Kritosaurus navajovius

Corythosaurus casuarius

it would have been most useful to look across the herd and identify members of one's own species by the shape of the upraised head.

Skeletal evidence indicates that hadrosaurs were equipped with sharp ears and may have had very loud voices with which to communicate with one another (perhaps, in some cases, by resonating trumpetlike within the enlarged nasal passages). In addition, their orbits were large, implying sharp vision, and as we have seen, the sense of smell was acute. They appear to have moved in herds across open savannah and along the edges of forests, keeping a sharp watch for tyrannosaurids and perhaps communicating with one another by hoots and whistles and visual displays. A recent find in Montana suggests that the family life of hadrosaurs was complex, perhaps arranged around crèches in which the young of several parents were protected by one or two adults. In Montana, perhaps fifteen baby hadrosaurs were found together with the skeleton of an adult that had very likely been guarding them. Some Mesozoic catastrophe overtook them where they lay, presenting us with a family tableau the like of which is all too rare among the dinosaurs.

Examination of hadrosaur "mummies" shows us that their skin was leathery and uninsulated, like that of mammals of similar mass, rather than covered by scales or any sort of armor. The texture of the skin was rougher on the upper part of the animal than on the underside, perhaps implying lighter coloring underneath as in most land (and aquatic) animals.

The hadrosaurs reached the apex of their success just before the end of the Mesozoic. Discarding the "great fossil Lizard" model of the amphibious duck-bill, we find in the hadrosaurs creatures that, for all their size and mass, must have presented an appearance of grace akin to that of their ecologic counterparts the antelope. Combining fleet-footedness with acute hearing, sharp eyes, and a keen olfactory sense, both hadrosaurs and antelope have made the most of their ability to digest silicaceous plant matter and thus have enjoyed unequaled success in their respective times.

The group of dinosaurs containing the hypsilophodonts, camptosaurs, iguanodonts, and hadrosaurs is known as suborder Ornithopoda, the "bird-feet," because of their usually three-toed, birdlike hind feet. This suborder contained one more small family, the pachycephalosaurs or "fat-headed lizards," so called because the bones of their braincases are massively thickened to produce a domed effect in the skull as a whole. The reason for this specialization remains a mystery. The pachycephalosaurs were fast bipeds like the rest of the ornithopods, and it is possible that they dashed head-down into thick vegetation when threatened by predators. This method of escape is used in modern times by cassowaries and guinea fowl, birds sporting similarly shockproof bone helmets.

The pachycephalosaur *Stegoceras,* "plate-head," and its brain, whose small size belies the tenured-professor-like appearance of the animal's domed head.

CERATOPSIA

One close Lower Cretaceous relative of *Camptosaurus* and *Iguanodon*, an animal sharing most of their dental, digestive, and other characteristics, began a process of diversion from that basic ornithopod plan to found one of the most impressively successful of dinosaur suborders, including the last of the dinosaurs to die out at the end of the Mesozoic. *Psittacosaurus* was a small ornithopod about two meters long, a biped that from the neck down was almost identical to *Iguanodon* except for its forefeet, which lacked the pointed thumb. The ornithopod beak, however, was modified in *Psittacosaurus* to become a heavy hook like a parrot's beak (hence the name, "parrot-lizard"). In response to this change the entire skull of *Psittacosaurus* was deepened, losing the characteristic ornithopod flat-headed look and becoming quite massive in the process.

The diet change resulting in the development of *Psittacosaurus*'s large beak must have been to tougher, more fibrous plants than those for which the older ornithopods were designed. Indeed, *Psittacosaurus*, with the growing jaw musculature associated with its deep skull, must surely have been able to burrow its head rodentlike into the heart of the thorniest cycad. In the usual fashion, the more the parrot-beaked dinosaurs found to eat, the larger they grew. Their growing biting and chewing specializations resulted in gradual enlargement of the head, to a point where they were no longer able to stand on their hind legs.

When next we meet this line in the fossil record, it is in the form of *Protoceratops* of the Mongolian Cretaceous. Founder of the mighty suborder Ceratopsia (the "horn-faces"), the aptly named *Protoceratops* is a permanent quadruped, its head having carried the specialization of *Psittacosaurus* to an extreme. *Protoceratops* was a small dinosaur about two and a half meters in length; however, of this length more than a quarter is the massive skull, whose long jaws and hooked beak were operated by muscles so huge that the bones of the back of the skull are extended rearward in a long arc to provide a surface to which the muscles were attached. This arc or frill extends over the animal's shoulders, doubling the length of the head and reducing its mobility, so that *Protoceratops* was effectively neckless. The powerful cheek muscles increased in size and the shearing teeth in number to several hundred as whatever it was that this preposterous animal ate grew tougher. The thing could happily have eaten solid wood!

Whatever it was that these powerful biters liked the most, there must have been plenty of it, for the descendants of some genus very like *Protoceratops* evolved consistently in the direction of greater size, especially in the skull, ultimately producing a number of species with the largest heads ever seen in terrestrial animals. All ceratopsians, whether or not they had horns (*Protoceratops* possessed only the suggestion of one), sported a great bony frill at the rear of the head, against which the giant muscles of the jaws operated. As this incredible chewing apparatus increased in size, the muscles required to support and operate it grew faster, so that the frill generally increased in length. Early

---

Psittacosaurus, with its heavy head and chewing equipment, was close to the ancestry of the Ceratopsia.

Protoceratops, a primitive ceratopsian, had a large head nearly covered with bulging muscles for chewing. The weight of this head was responsible for the animal's return to quadrupedalism.

---

restorations portray ceratopsians as having been "protected from neck wounds" by a broad, concave frill extending along the back; this is inaccurate, however, for the primary function of the frill was as a muscle attachment. The great temporal muscles responsible for the animals' marvelous shearing ability bulged across the front surface of the frill, while its rear border was obscured by the massive neck muscles that supported and turned the huge head. Thus the restoration of ceratopsians in this book may appear unfamiliar to many old-time enthusiasts of ceratopsian dinosaurs.

As the ceratopsians progressed through the later Cretaceous, they experienced moderate radiation in form as they ate a greater variety of . . . what? Tree trunks? With increase in size came corresponding increase in the capacity of the astonishing parrot-beaked chewing apparatus. The jaws became longer and longer, sporting layer upon layer of hundreds of fast-growing replaceable teeth in long bladelike rows, while the beak itself became stouter and the cheek muscles stronger. All of this increased the head weight, causing the ceratopsians to lose much of the agility that graced their ancestors. In response—sharing their world, as they did, with fast and fearsome predators—the ceratopsians began to sport the various horns for which they are named. Some, such as the medium-sized *Monoclonius* (about four meters long), contented themselves with a single rhinoceroslike horn on the nose, while others, such as the well-

Triceratops, one of the largest and last of the Ceratopsia, showing some of the remarkable adaptations for chewing characteristic of the family. *Left*: The skull of *Triceratops* with attendant musculature. *Far left*: *Triceratops* as a "great fossil Lizard," with the muscles of cheeks and rear of skull omitted in the classic restoration. *Right*: Cross section of the jaws of *Triceratops*, showing the perpetually replaced teeth that permitted nonstop chewing of highly fibrous woody matter.

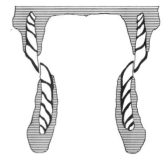

known *Triceratops* of the Upper Cretaceous, evolved up to three great horns on the front of the face.

Associated with the increase in length of the ceratopsian skull came various embellishments of its frill. *Monoclonius*'s frill was embossed with knobs regularly spaced around the rim, while its cousin, the aptly named *Styracosaurus* ("spiked lizard"), possessed a frill impressively decorated with six long spines that projected over the animal's back. In some forms the frill retained a large opening on either side, reducing the area for attachment of muscles, so that as these animals grew in size, their frills were forced to undergo a disproportionate enlargement around the rim to compensate. At the apex of this line of evolution is *Torosaurus*, the "bull-lizard," whose skull is longer than that of any other land animal, reaching a length of two and a half meters. In others the opening was reduced, so that the entire area of the frill served as an area for muscle attachment; in these forms, of which *Triceratops* is the last in the fossil record, the frill remained relatively short, the head more mobile.

The primitive *protoceratops* is particularly interesting in that it was found in all stages of development, from egg to adult. The manner in which these animals appear with their eggs suggests that numbers of adults laid eggs in closely spaced nests in a crèche area. These eggs were about twenty centimeters long and covered with a textured shell, and were laid in groups of fifteen or more in concentric fashion, as if the mother *Protoceratops* circled the nest as she laid them.

The skull of newly hatched *Protoceratops* shows a relatively small frill which grew rapidly in length as the animal exercised it in chewing his woody food. The newborn ceratopsian must have been limited by his infantile chewing equipment to the softest foods, perhaps being fed regurgitated food by adults and moving gradually to tougher food as his shearing apparatus grew. Young ceratopsians were nearly helpless animals, small and slow, and they probably enjoyed parental protection until they were old enough to move with the herd and share its food.

In all the ceratopsians equipped with horns, these structures occur in both male and female. This indicates that the horns were weapons of defense against the peerless predators of the late Cretaceous, rather than implements of intraspecific combat like the antlers of stags. Ecologically, the ceratopsians, especially later models, appear to have resembled bovids such as bison and buffalo rather than the rhinoceroses with which they are often compared. There is evidence

Some ceratopsian types: *Top*: *Chasmosaurus,* with its greatly elongated frill. *Middle*: *Styracosaurus,* equipped with defensive neck spines. *Bottom*: *Torosaurus,* with a skull eight feet long.

that these animals moved in vast herds, alongside which, no doubt, tyrannosaurids moved in small groups or pairs, hoping to spot the ill or unprotected for a quick meal. It is unlikely that a tyrannosaurid could have successfully taken on a healthy adult *Triceratops*, any more than a lion might hope to bring down a healthy Cape buffalo, and the presence of the horns suggests that herds of ceratopsians, like bovids, may have formed a collective and thorny front between their hornless, defenseless young and the ever-watchful predators.

With their staggering chewing machinery, their ability to eat just about anything vegetable, and their advanced social organization, ceratopsians were the dominant open-land herbivores of the later Cretaceous. The efficiency of their design must have had enormous impact on the ecology of which they were part, their vast numbers and collective appetite probably sharply reducing the number of niches available to lesser archosaurs. Thus the triumph of the ceratopsians may have been responsible for some of the disappearances of archosaur genera reflected in the Lance deposits of the Upper Cretaceous. At any rate, the ceratopsians survived most other dinosaurs and were still moving about in great numbers at the very end of the Mesozoic, the last to fall to whatever it was that ended the era.

In retrospect, one is tempted to miss these marvels of digestive efficiency. Imagine the convenience of purchasing an egg of *Triceratops*, hatching it, and feeding the growing animal with inexpensive foods such as abandoned buildings, sawdust, old newspapers, or dead trees, perhaps spiced with an unused railroad trestle or stand of scrub oak, until it reached its maximum size of seven meters in length and some nine tons' mass (about twice that of a large elephant). An unsurpassable draft animal, or, if you are hungry, a lot of beef! And if you're squeamish about eating dinosaur, take a close look at the next chicken on your table. . . .

HELMETS, MACES, AND MAIL

From some ornithopod ancestor also rose two lines of herbivorous dinosaurs specializing in the consumption of low, tender plants such as mosses, cycad seedlings, and the like. This diet naturally forced the posture of these animals toward the ground and quadrupedalism, and to make up for their loss of speed and agility, they tended to evolve defensive implements such as spiny shells, clublike tails, and bodily armor.

The earliest such animals known to us is *Scelidosaurus* ("side lizard") of Lower Jurassic England. Although its hind legs were still considerably longer than the forelegs, *Scelidosaurus* was down on all fours for good in its quest for the many small plants on which it fed. Its head was carried close to the ground, the spine rising to a high point at the pelvis, giving the animal an arched appearance as it ambled along. This peaceful creature was defended only by a set of bony armor plates, separate from the rest of the skeleton and embedded in the skin along its back and sides. To discourage predators that tended to attack the spinal column, the plates along the back were raised like large sawteeth.

Unfortunately, *Scelidosaurus*'s armor wasn't really enough; the behavior of predators evolved around this feeble attempt at self-protection, and *Scelidosaurus* survived only a relatively short time. In all probability descended from this genus, however, are the famous stegosaurs of the Upper Jurassic, who relied on specialization of the spinal armor to achieve a measure of protection from the contemporary megalosaurs.

It is still uncertain, despite the wealth of stegosaur remains available to us, exactly how this spinal armor worked. Most of the several genera of stegosaurs ("plated lizards") possessed modifications of tail armor in the form of several pairs of stout spines. Although it is obvious that the tail was flailed at attacking predators in an attempt to impale them on the spines, it is hard to see how this was done; the spines pointed upward, and the tail must have flailed sideways if a standing stegosaur hoped to knock down a predator. In addition, the armor along the rest of the spine was also vertical, whether it took the form of great triangular bone plates or spikes similar to those on the tail. Some workers have gone so far as to suggest that these plates and spines were either sexual ornaments or supports for a solar-heating apparatus of some sort; how-

The stegosaur *Kentrosaurus,* showing the spines and plates along the back characteristic of the family.

ever, they occur in both male and female stegosaurs and, standing in double rows as they do, would block the sun from one another and support a miserably small sun-gathering surface for such large animals as stegosaurs.

Perhaps, in the manner of gigantic hedgehogs, the stegosaurs fell on their sides and curled up when confronted by predators; in this case the tail would swing horizontally outward when sprung from the coiled stegosaur, aiming its deadly spikes at the legs and abdomen of a bipedal predator. In such a recumbent stegosaur the spinal armor would create a prickly rim to the nearly circular form of the animal, certainly discouraging carelessness on the part of predators.

However, this defense didn't work well enough ultimately. That the

Below: Stegosaurs may have defended themselves by flopping onto their sides, presenting sawtooth armor on all sides. *Opposite, top: Scelidosaurus*, a primitive stegosaur from the Lower Jurassic. *Middle: Syrmosaurus*, a primitive ankylosaur with spiky armor and a tail like a double-bitted ax. Old restorations show these animals dragging their tails on the ground, rendering these appendages useless in defense; more likely, however, the tail was carried well off the ground. *Bottom*: The ankylosaur *Polecanthus*, a spiny form superficially resembling a stegosaur.

specialization was less than entirely effective is shown by the fact that the stegosaurs are the only dinosaur suborder to have become extinct well before the end of the Mesozoic. The last stegosaurs died during the early Cretaceous, whereas their relatives continued the dinosaur hegemony for more than 60 million years.

One reason for the decline of the stegosaurs may have been the ascent of some of their relatives, the ankylosaurs ("stiffened lizards"), a group whose upper body was covered by nodes and plates of bony armor. Possibly descended from a close relative of *Scelidosaurus*, the ankylosaurs also specialized in eating small tender plants and, like the stegosaurs, reflected this diet in weak teeth and a posture set close to the ground on four legs. Ankylosaurs eschewed specialized spinal armor and opted for a very low profile, short legs, and an armadillolike mail coat stretching from the head to the tip of the tail. This latter appendage was usually armed with a stout club or spiked mace. The entire effect leads us to believe that the ankylosaurs simply crouched to the ground when attacked, waiting until the predator approached close enough to be belted with the massive tail.

Like the other dinosaurs, ankylosaurs descended from bipeds; their hind legs remain somewhat longer than the forelegs, so that their armor shells have a domed shape. However, these leg lengths are actually more nearly equal than in most dinosaurs, a development related to the need to hide the entire body under the cuirass. The head could be withdrawn a bit in the manner of a turtle; in addition, it too was covered with bone plates, giving these animals a blunt-headed appearance.

An early ankylosaur genus reflecting many of these specializations is the Lower Cretaceous Mongolian *Syrmosaurus*. This animal possessed a stiffened tail whose tip was enlarged into a weighty double-bladed axlike club. The entire back and sides of the animal were regularly studded with bone knobs and plates, presenting rather the aspect of a neat pile of rocks on four legs. Later forms expanded on this armor, adding long spines on the back or along the sides to make them difficult to turn over. In the process the ankylosaurs became tremendously heavy and lower and lower to hide the soft underparts. By the late Cretaceous the ankylosaurs were completely encased in interlocking armor, from head to tail and extending below the animals' sides, even meeting to encircle the tail completely. In all these later forms the tail was equipped with a mace of some sort that was more than capable of breaking the leg of a carnosaur. With their great mass and low configuration, these animals continued to munch the smaller, tenderer plants in safety until they joined their cousins in the mass extinctions at the end of the Mesozoic.

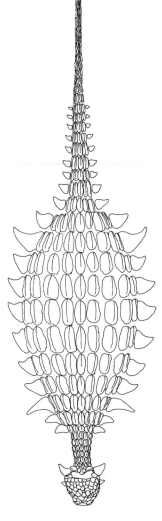

Armor of *Ankylosaurus* from above.

PTEROSAURIA

Dinosaurs were not the only beings to have benefited from the endothermy developed by the Triassic thecodonts. Some such primitive archosaur, insulated against cold and lightly built, seems to have taken to climbing about and gliding from rocks and trees like modern flying squirrels. Since they were climbers, they did not lose any fingers, as did many of their cousins the dinosaurs; indeed, through the eons the fourth finger became a great long strut, providing rigidity for a long flap of skin stretching from the tip of the finger to the body. With this structure these animals ultimately learned to fly.

Being the high-energy little animals they were, pterosaurs ("wing lizards") possessed insulation with which to maintain body warmth. By the time pterosaurs were fully airborne, they were densely coated with fur, which actually left an impression in some of the finer pterosaur fossils, so that it can be seen today.

The primitive archosaurian forearm (*middle*) evolved into wings in two independent ways: the pterosaur wing (*top*) and the bird wing (*bottom*).

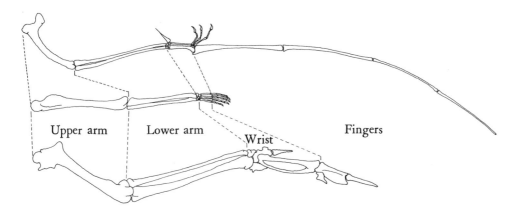

Upper arm   Lower arm   Wrist   Fingers

The air was a new habitat for vertebrates, and with no competition, the early pterosaurs proliferated. While some were no larger than modern robins, others achieved the probable upper limit in size for an earthly animal flier. Indeed, some late Cretaceous forms may have had wingspreads of fifteen meters; these were literally living sails, great, lovely open-ocean beings weighing only a few kilograms that soared for months, perhaps, like giant albatrosses, across the Mesozoic seas.

In addition to their wings, the pterosaurs exhibit the complete constellation of adaptations appropriate to airborne vertebrates. Their hollow bones, when sectioned, show the Haversian canals of endothermy, while the centers of the larger of these bones were filled with extensions of the respiratory system as in birds. As in birds, the sternum (breastbone) was enlarged and equipped

Pteranodon, a Cretaceous pterosaur, may have had a wingspread of fifteen meters and probably lived a life rather like that of modern albatrosses on the open sea.

with a keel for the mounting of muscles of flight, while the areas of the brain involved with sight, balance, and other flight-essential senses and skills are enlarged, so that the braincase spreads out behind the eyes. In almost all ways the pterosaurs show parallelism with the birds and bats in flying adaptations.

Unfortunately for the pterosaurs, however, the dinosaurian flight plan, as first exhibited in the Jurassic in birds, was more efficient. Unlike the pterosaurs, the bird ancestors entered a sky already populated by flying vertebrates. To overcome this disadvantage the birds evolved their wing from their tough and flexible insulating feathers, rather than from a delicate flap of skin. Even a

Pterosaurs evolved into a number of airborne niches before their place was usurped by birds during the Cretaceous. *Above*: The primitive *Dimorphodon*, "two-kinds-of-teeth," probably an insect-eater. *Below*: *Dorygnathus*, probably a fish-eater.

small tear in the wing membrane of a pterosaur meant his end, for the damage was unlikely to heal, and he was grounded. Once grounded, pterosaurs were unequipped to run. Indeed, it is hard to see how these animals got about at all on the ground. Birds, on the other hand, retained their dinosaurian running hind legs, with which they might escape when grounded. When the feathers of a bird wing were damaged, they grew in again rapidly; in the meantime the bird resumed a terrestrial-dinosaur running existence.

By the end of the Cretaceous, therefore, the air was occupied by many species of true birds but few remaining pterosaurs. Of all the Mesozoic forms we have discussed, the pterosaurs seem in many ways the most alien. So new were their remains to human experience that their discoverers did not believe these could represent flying animals, preferring to demote them to swimming status. Later workers, finding fossils of pterosaurs retaining marks of their hair, suggested that these animals were actually flying marsupial bats. Only recently have the pterosaurs been promoted by paleontologists from the ranks of the great fossil lizard to their proper position as endotherms among their archosaurian cousins.

WHAT HAPPENED?

So what happened? If the dinosaurs and pterosaurs were as progressive as we have been saying throughout this book, where did they go? Why are they no longer here, while we are, if they were so admirably designed?

It is a certainty that the dinosaurs (with the exception of birds) and pterosaurs died out completely at the end of the Mesozoic. So abrupt is their disappearance that it may have taken less than a million years, an instant in geological time. It may have been a far shorter process, lasting only a few centuries, or even a day. We may never know how long the extinctions took, but we do know this. The dinosaurs dominated the planet's land and air to the very end of the Cretaceous, showing their greatest diversity and vigor right at the end. Then, wham! there is a space in the fossil record in which no large land animal is to be found, a space lasting for some millions of years. Finally, mammals began slowly to radiate into the many niches left vacant by the dinosaurs. As a class we are still relative newcomers in the dominant position, having done only about 60 million years to the dinosaurs' 165 million.

The theories attempting to explain the end of the Mesozoic have been diverse and wondrous, filling many massy tomes. As soon as the European world was convinced that there had been whole orders of animals on this planet which no longer existed, a number of learned gents sprang forth and suggested that the fossils represented populations of God's mistakes, which He had erased in a series of violent piques before perfecting His art in Man, the image of His Person. These acts of God might have been performed with the aid of comets, objects still regarded with superstitious awe in the time of the first discovery of dinosaur remains. The comet suggestion was said to be borne out by the contorted poses in which many dinosaur skeletons were discovered; the fact that the neck was curved sharply over the animals' back showed that the dinosaurs were struck down "while looking at a great Comet"!

As more data came in, it was discovered that not only the great fossil lizards but also many land plants, mammals, birds, and reptiles had disappeared. In addition, the marine fossil record shows that life in the ocean was similarly affected; many phytoplankton (microscopic floating plants), nearly the entire order of higher mollusks called ammonites, the entire assemblage of marine reptiles excepting turtles, and a host of other forms also disappeared at the end of the Mesozoic.

Some people have suggested that these varied extinct forms were the result of an imagined tendency of living forms to become "senile," to reach a point where their "germ plasm" is no longer able to function properly. The signs

---

An aptly named dinocephalian ("horrible-headed") therapsid predator, belonging to a group of animals transitional between reptiles and mammals. When these endotherms and early dinosaurs first met, the therapsids became extinct in the ensuing competition for supremacy. Their mammalian descendants were forced into a peripheral position in the terrestrial ecosystem until the dinosaurs disappeared at the end of the Mesozoic.

of great specialization in some animals were taken as representative of this process; ammonites, for instance, acquired many strange shell shapes before the Mesozoic's end, and the crests of the hadrosaurs, the frills of ceratopsians, and the huge size of many of these animals were considered evidence that something had gone wrong with evolution. However, as we have seen, such specializations in the dinosaurs were precisely the qualities guaranteeing their success. There is no basis in reality to the "racial senility" theory.

Others have suggested that the rise of flowering plants, with their use of alkaloid poisons to defend themselves against herbivores, contributed to the extinction of dinosaurs. The aforementioned contortions in the necks of fossil dinosaurs have been posed as evidence of death from poisoning. However, these contorted dinosaur necks are simply the result of post-mortem contraction of the muscles raising the neck, contractions which also occur after death in birds—witness the "bishop's crook" of the chicken neck. Besides, flowering plants had been evolving since the early Cretaceous, and their success was simultaneous with that of hadrosaurs, ankylosaurs, and ceratopsians in the late Cretaceous, an indication that the dinosaurs profited well from the new plants. Also, there is in this theory no explanation for marine extinctions, so the flowering-plant theory must follow the others we have examined into the realm of entertaining speculation.

In the old days it was suggested that the mammals of the Mesozoic drove the dinosaurs into extinction by being warm-blooded, while the dinosaurs were, of course, great fossil lizards. Possessing all the advantages of the noble station of endothermy, these minute mammals were said, for instance, to have eaten archosaurian eggs until the dinosaurs were no more. Again, however, there is no explanation for the marine extinctions. Also, as we have already said, mammal ancestors had evolved endothermy by the Mid-Triassic in the form of unearthly-looking sprawling creatures called therapsids; if they possessed such an advantage over the dinosaurs, they should have conquered the planet long before. The fossil record shows us that the tall, fast archosaurs quickly eliminated the ungainly therapsids when first they met, so that through the rest of the Mesozoic the mammals remained tiny creepers living a life of touch and smell in dark places, while the archosaurs branched out and became sharp-eyed, nimble, and dominant. So mammals didn't do it—in fact, after the close of the Mesozoic, several million years elapsed before the mammals began to creep out and experiment with new roles.

In the popular literature dinosaurs are thought of as stupid, and this stupidity has been said to have led to their disappearance. Forgetting for the moment that this theory also neglects the other extinctions of the time, we can digress for a look at the dinosaurian intellect, a fascinating subject for speculation. For nearly as long as we have known about dinosaurs, we have marveled at the fact that, of all known vertebrates, these animals had the smallest brains in proportion to their bodies. This has inevitably led to the conclusion that dinosaurs, in all their diversity, were impressively dimwitted. However, judging from their brain cavities, the very earliest dinosaurs had brains of almost the same size as those of their descendants 165 million years later, indicating that such small brains were quite adequate through that immense interval.

In discussing the intelligence of dinosaurs we must keep in mind the structure of the archosaur nervous system, one wired rather differently than our own. Both mammalian and archosaurian brains are built on a reptilian plan, since both of these groups are descended from reptiles. In mammals the brain is large and close to the ground, supported by the forefeet. The mammals emerged into endothermy as quadrupeds and have continued so for some 230 or more million years. Only in human beings has true bipedalism occurred among mammals.

In archosaurs, on the other hand, bipedal posture occurred simultaneously with the appearance of endothermy. The brain, carried well forward of the center of gravity by a strong forward lean, remained small and light. Many functions of coordination involving the limbs occur far down the spinal cord, which reflects this division of labor with marked swellings at appropriate points along its length. It is likely, for example, that the complex motions of walking and running were governed in large part by a swelling of the spinal cord in the pelvic area of dinosaurs, called the sacral plexus. This swelling persists in birds and is in part responsible for chickens' "running with their heads cut off" after execution. In certain dinosaurs (and certain modern birds) the sacral plexus was larger than the actual brain, prompting an otherwise forgotten American poet to suggest that:

> *This creature had two sets of brains;*
> *One in his head (the usual place),*
> *The other at his spinal base.*

A lesser such swelling, the brachial plexus, occurs in the shoulder area of the spine and deals with movements of the forelegs. It is likely that elementary metabolic functions such as digestion were also more independent of the brain in dinosaurs than in mammals. This arrangement probably permitted quicker reactions than would have been possible in some of the very long sauropods, had they possessed a highly centralized nervous system like our own.

Much of the volume of the brain proper in dinosaurs was probably devoted to coordination of highly organized instinctual behavior such as nest building and the raising of young. Again, we may look at the birds for comparison. Possessing brains almost identical to those of their dinosaurian antecedents, birds differ from us in the lack of a highly evolved cerebral cortex, the seat in mammals of intelligent behavior. In spite of this difference, some birds must be called intelligent in almost anyone's reckoning; ravens and crows of family Corvidae, for instance, can duplicate feats of problem solving as well as some

---

The brain and spinal cord of an archosaur, showing the brachial and sacral plexi through which movements of the limbs were coordinated.

of the higher primates (monkeys, etc.), our own order. In some laboratory tests, such birds consistently outthink dogs and cats with brains many times greater in volume and, as anyone who has ever maintained a crow as a pet knows, sometimes approach humans in such "intelligent" manifestations as sense of humor and attempts at deception.

In these intelligent birds a cross section of the brain reveals great development of the *corpus striatum*, a layered volume of nerve tissue within the cerebrum. The *corpus striatum* originated in reptiles and persists in mammals as a small nerve center buried deep in the brain. The archosaurs, however, appear to have concentrated the functions of problem solving and other intelligent behaviors in this region rather than in the cerebral cortex as in mammals. The cortex in archosaurs appears to have been involved mainly with inborn behavior complexes, having lost almost all its problem-solving ability to the underlying *corpus striatum*, which is correspondingly enlarged.

So we see that the small dinosaur brain is not really indicative of intelligence or stupidity, but only of a nonmammalian nervous organization. The vast success of dinosaurs suggests that their behavior was at least as complex as that of birds and probably approached in variety the behavior of mammals in cases where the ecologic functions of the two groups converge (as in megalosaurs and wolves). It is certain that much bird behavior is inborn, and it is probable that this was also the case among Mesozoic dinosaurs. However, we cannot get away with calling birds as a group stupid, and we must at last relegate our old visions of dunderheaded dinosaurs to the archives of interesting ideological relics.

To return to the subject of the Mesozoic extinctions, for years it has been suggested that cold ended the era. Many workers suggest that temperatures suddenly dropped around the world, perhaps in conjunction with a nearby supernova or a change in the sun's activity. As great fossil lizards, the dinosaurs wouldn't have had a chance in such conditions, but as the endotherms they really seem to have been, they should have been able to survive in some form. Those adapted to temperate and cooler climates should have lived on, as should the smaller, insulated forms. Too, the evolution of deciduous trees long before the end of the Cretaceous indicates that seasons were well delineated in those days, implying that many of the immensely successful late Cretaceous dinosaurs were perfectly well able to handle winter conditions where necessary. Also this theory does not explain the extinctions of many mammals, birds, and all marine reptiles with the exception of turtles, or of the many other living things that disappeared at the end of the Mesozoic.

In the freewheeling tradition of paleontological speculation, the author feels entitled to toss his own pet theory into the ring. Examination of the animal genera most affected by the Mesozoic extinctions presents an interesting parallel among them: they represent almost all the most energy-consumptive, conspicuous, and active beasts of their time, both in terrestrial and marine environments. In other words, almost all the animals at the tops of their food chains, those most likely to be affected by short-term changes in food supplies, disappeared from the planetary surface in one swell foop.

Since the extinction spared no class of animal on the basis of metabolism, we may rule out cold alone as the cause. A more widespread ecologic disruption seems to have occurred, and in many ways it seems as if this disruption affected mainly the photosynthetic process at the very base of the earthly bioenergetic system. Such an occurrence would instantly strike at those animals that were most energy-intensive. Highly active herbivores, and all that feed on them, would be reduced drastically in numbers. Animals, on the other hand, whose metabolic processes were slower (reptiles, which can go without food for long periods of time), or who burrowed and hibernated (early mammals), or who, because of small size and great mobility, could exploit the world's widely scattered remaining energy sources for a time (birds) might survive. In the seas, the disappearance of the dominant predators (marine reptiles and ammonites) would be a natural outcome of a drop in the amount of energy trapped in phytoplankton; those animals on a more intermediate level in the food chain, such as the jellyfish-eating sea turtles, might survive through the change.

The manner in which the photosynthetic process might be interrupted on a worldwide level could involve a dimming of the light reaching the earth's plants. Such a darkness need have lasted only a few months to strike down most of the animals that became extinct at the end of the Mesozoic, particularly the nonhibernating, nonburrowing, nonflying dinosaurs. If a dense cloud cover were raised—perhaps by the impact of a large bolide (meteorite), or by effects on the upper atmosphere caused by the explosion of a nearby star—the planetary temperature might *rise* somewhat owing to the greenhouse effect, in which dense clouds trap much of the sun's energy. However, in the ensuing dim light, the production of organic matter by plants would not be able to keep up with the eating done by the world's herbivores, and the living system would experience an unprecedented famine.

Plants, of course, are slow-going creatures with varying abilities to store energy through hard times in their roots, stems, leaves, or seeds; those plants accustomed to going dormant through cold seasons would be best equipped for surviving a period of darkness. There is some evidence that it was precisely these plants that did best at the end of the Cretaceous.

Whatever happened, the Paleocene epoch that opened the Cenozoic found the world a lonely place indeed, emptied as it was of all its more advanced animals. Surviving birds made a bid for the old dinosaur niches, producing a variety of large ground-dwelling forms, but these recidivist creatures lacked tails and forelimbs and could not withstand the eventual rise of the mammals. Gradually the planet's emptied niches began to fill again as mammals sniffed their way into the light. For 60 million years these opportunists experimented, eventually producing as great a variety of species as did their archosaurian predecessors.

Now the Cenozoic, too, appears to be in its final stages as the world undergoes yet another great extinction. From its peak only a few thousand years ago, the mammalian class has been sharply reduced in variety, with entire families following the dinosaurs into extinction. Between 60 thousand and 10 thousand years ago, more than half of the world's genera of larger mammals disappeared forever. During the same period most of the surviving mammalian predators underwent a reduction in size, a reflection of hard times for these survivors.

The current extinctions strikingly parallel those at the end of the Mesozoic in that they again occur in a geologically minute period of time, with all the most advanced and energy-consumptive animals extinct or threatened with extinction. In the sea, most of the largest fish and the entire ancient clan of whales face oblivion, while on land the higher predators—cats large and small, wild dogs, birds of prey, even crocodilians—all are rapidly disappearing. The few remaining large herds of herbivores in the Holarctic tundras and the African savannas are confined to "wildernesses" and "game preserves" to wait out their remaining years in neat sequestration.

These recent extinctions stem from a highly visible cause—the rise of *Homo sapiens*, the ultimate generalist whose niche spans the niches of thousands of other species. From his origins as a Pleistocene hunter equipped with fire to his present status as the only living form intentionally able to leave its earthly home, Man the Wise has had a solidly detrimental effect on the living system as a whole. Now, as human numbers press at the limits of our planet's capacity to support them, human ingenuity creates a host of new environmental stresses, any one of which may deliver the *coup de grâce* to the Cenozoic.

Our look at the Mesozoic offers us a lesson in the special fragility of advanced living things. In reviewing the early triumph and long success of the dinosaurs, we are primarily impressed with their efficiency and adaptability in the face of change. And in examining the sudden disappearance of these splendid animals, we are forced to look to our own time. Here we face responsibility as human beings, our unique responsibility for the continuation or termination of the Cenozoic Era. Unlike the dinosaurs, we have a choice in the matter.

Acetabulum   The hollow in which the thighbone articulates with the pelvis, the center of mass in bipedal dinosaurs.

Allosaurus   A megalosaur whose name, "weird lizard," refers to the fact that its discoverers had never seen anything of the like before.

Ammonite   An extinct marine mollusk, related to the octopus and squid, in which the head and tentacles protruded from a shell. The ammonites disappeared, along with many other living forms, at the end of the Mesozoic.

Amnion   A membrane in the eggs of terrestrial vertebrates, in which moisture (amniotic fluid) necessary for the life of the embryo is contained.

Ankylosaur   Any of a family ("stiffened lizards") of ornithischian dinosaurs which were quadrupeds equipped with bony armor.

Archaeopteryx   "Old wing," a small coelurosaurian dinosaur whose feathers appear in fossils, leading early paleontologists to believe it was actually a bird.

Archosauria   A proposed class of vertebrates containing the birds, dinosaurs, crocodilians, and certain other forms now extinct. Archosaurs were formerly listed as a subclass of class Reptilia, based mainly on common skeletal features, while birds were given a separate class, Aves.

Arthropoda   A phylum of animals including insects, crustaceans, spiders, and other animals with jointed armor on the outside of the body, rather than an internal skeleton as in vertebrates. Arthropods are the dominant phylum of animals, outnumbering in known species all other animals combined.

Aves   Birds. Formerly included in a class of their own, birds now appear to be dinosaurs specialized for flight.

Biomass   Matter incorporated in the living system at any given moment. Biomass is created by plants through the process of photosynthesis and is distributed around the planet by the activity of animals, water, and other agencies before it breaks down and returns to the nonliving state, to be recycled yet again in the process of plant metabolism.

Bipedal	"Two-footed," as men and birds.
Brachiosaurus	The "arm lizard," a sauropod genus whose forelimbs were longer than the hindlimbs, a condition rare among dinosaurs.
Brontosaurus	The "thunder lizard," a sauropod genus typifying the great size and mass of the suborder.
Camarasaurus	The "chambered lizard," a medium-sized sauropod, so called because of the hollowed-out structure of its skeleton.
Camptosaurus	The "flexible lizard," a primitive ornithopod dinosaur.
Carnivore	A flesh-eating animal.
Carnosauria	The heavy-predator infraorder of dinosaurs, including teratosaurs, megalosaurs, and tyrannosaurs.
Ceratopsia	The "horn-faced" suborder of dinosaurs.
Chordata	A phylum of animals possessing, at some point in their development, a notochord, a stiffening structure running the length of the body. Chordates and arthropods are the two most highly evolved animal phyla and the most successful in the conquest of land.
Coelophysis	The "hollow-boned" dinosaur, a small coelurosaur of the Upper Triassic of New Mexico.
Coelurosauria	The light-predator infraorder of dinosaurs, from which birds are believed to have descended.
Compsognathus	The "elegant-jawed" dinosaur, a small coelurosaur closely related to *Archaeopteryx*.
Conifer	Any of those woody plants such as pines, spruces, cedars, etc., which were the dominant land flora during much of the early Mesozoic and which remain highly successful to this day.
Convergence	The process in which distantly related organisms with similar life-styles tend to approach one another in form and function. A classic example of convergence is the similarity in appearance of fish, dolphins, and ichthyosaurs, vertebrates adapted to marine life but descended from very dissimilar antecedents.
Crèche	A communal nursery where parents share the tasks of raising and protecting young. A familiar crèche is the parent-operated day-care center for urban human young. Many dinosaurs may have raised their defenseless young in crèches.
Cycad	Any of an order of plants resembling fernlike palms, sharing dominance of the Mesozoic with the conifers. Cycads are tough, thorny plants, the efficiency of whose armor is reflected in the astounding grinding dentitions of many dinosaurs that fed on them. Cycads are today restricted in distribution to the tropics.
Diplodocus	The "double-beamed," a long, thin sauropod, so called because of the massive supports of its vertebral column.
Dromaeosaur	Any of the "emu-lizards," advanced coelurosaurs, many of which were equipped with modified inner hind toes for kicking their prey to death.

Ecology	The study of the distribution of matter, space, energy, and time by the living system or parts thereof.
Ectotherm	An animal whose body heat is maintained by conditions in its environment rather than by internal physiologic processes; a "cold-blooded" animal.
Endotherm	An animal whose body heat is maintained by internal processes; a "warm-blooded" animal.
Euparkeria	A small primitive thecodont archosaur capable of running on its hind legs occasionally.
Fauna	The assemblage of animal life inhabiting an ecosystem.
Fossil	Something that is "dug up," specifically, traces of organisms preserved by geologic activity.
Geology	The study of the structure and evolution of the planet Earth.
Ginkgo	A genus of trees of which only one species, *Ginkgo biloba,* survives today. During the Mesozoic the family Ginkgoaceae was widespread, serving as food for many browsing animals of the time. Although native only to Asia today, *Ginkgo biloba* may be found along the streets of large cities worldwide, having been transplanted because of its resistance to urban pollutants. This "living fossil" is interesting in that its seeds are fertilized by swimming spermlike antherozoids rather than by passive pollen, as is the case in more advanced plants.
Gorgosaurus	The "horrible lizard," a smallish tyrannosaurid.
Hadrosauridae	The family of ornithischian dinosaurs whose members are commonly called "duckbills" because of their long flat snouts. Hadrosaurs were mainly upland browsers, many growing to large size—"hadrosaur" means "big lizard."
Herbivore	A plant-eating animal.
Hypsilophodon	A primitive ornithischian whose name means "high-crested tooth." *Hypsilophodon* is close to the form from which all other Ornithischia descended.
Ichthyosaur	"Fish-lizard," any of a group of reptiles that adopted a marine existence, converging with fish and dolphins in external appearance.
Iguanodontidae	The family of ornithischian dinosaurs whose members possessed shearing teeth supposed by their discoverer, Gideon Mantell, to resemble the teeth of living iguana lizards. "Iguanodon" means "iguana-tooth."
Kentrosaurus	The "pointed lizard," a stegosaur equipped with defensive spines down its back.
Larva	An immature stage in an animal's life history, as the pollywog of a toad, differing from the adult in at least one characteristic other than mere size.
Limnoscelis	A genus of primitive reptiles of the Lower Permian. From this, or a similar form, all higher reptiles and both mammals and archosaurs are descended. *Limnoscelis* means "scaly swamp-dweller."

Living system	Life, considered as a unitary process; the interconnected assemblage of beings and activities of which the biosphere is composed.
Longisquamata	A primitive "long-scaled" archosaur whose body covering may have insulated it against heat loss.
Mammalia	A class of vertebrates equipped with mammary glands, from which milk is fed to the young. Mammals are endotherms and are usually equipped with hairy bodily insulation.
Megalosaur	Any of the family Megalosauridae, "great lizards," named after Dean Buckland's original "great fossil Lizard." Megalosaurs were the large carnivores of the Jurassic.
Metabolism	The total activity of a living organism, in which food is assimilated, waste excreted, tissue created, energy manipulated, and reproduction accomplished.
Mineralization	A process in which a buried organism, or part of one, is preserved through replacement of its tissues by minerals in solution; sometimes called fossilization.
Monoclonius	A "one-horned" ceratopsian dinosaur.
Mosasaur	The "Meuse lizard," a large extinct marine lizard related to modern monitors, named after the River Meuse, near which its fossils were first discovered in Belgium.
Niche	The position of an organism in an ecologic system; often described as a volume delimited by parameters such as form, function, food, etc.
Orbit	In vertebrates, the opening in the skull in which the eyeball is seated.
Ornithischia	A dinosaur order whose hips resemble superficially those of birds, hence the name "bird-hips." Ornithischia were entirely herbivorous and very successful in the consumption of tough, fibrous vegetation.
Ornithomimidae	A family of coelurosaurian dinosaurs of remarkably birdlike appearance, hence the name, "bird-mimics." Ornithomimids were about the size and build of modern ostriches and were extremely sharp of eye and fleet of foot.
Ornithopoda	An ornithischian suborder, the "bird-feet," containing the hadrosaurs, iguanodonts, camptosaurs, and pachycephalosaurs. So called because their hind feet resembled those of birds.
Ornithosuchus	The "bird-crocodile," a lightly built bipedal thecodont. From some such animal the dinosaurs are believed to have descended.
Pachycephalosaur	Any of a small ornithopod family of "thick-headed" dinosaurs whose skull bones were extremely massive, perhaps to protect the brain from impact of some sort.
Paleontology	The study of life in the past.
Parasaurolophus	"Sort of a crested lizard," a crested hadrosaur whose bony head adornment swept backward in a long curve beyond the skull.
Pariesaur	The "wall-lizard," a group of primitive herbivorous reptiles, some of which achieved large size.

Pectoral girdle	The bones associating the forelimbs with the rest of the body in terrestrial vertebrates; also called the shoulder girdle.
Pelvic girdle	The bones associating the hind legs with the rest of the body in vertebrates; also called the hip girdle.
Pelycosaur	Any of an order of extinct reptiles ancestral to therapsids and mammals, the "bowl lizards," so called because of the conformation of their pelvic girdles.
Phytoplankton	Tiny plants floating at the surface of the world's bodies of water, responsible for most of the photosynthetic fueling of the aquatic living systems.
Phrysonoma	A genus of lizards inhabiting the warmer parts of the American Southwest and highly adapted for desert life. These lizards are flat and thorny; the name *Phrysonoma* means "toad-body," and is also reflected in the common name, "horned toad."
Plateosaurus	The "flat lizard," a genus of prosauropods.
Plesiosauridae	A family of aquatic reptiles of the Mesozoic usually characterized by a long neck and tail affixed to a flat, streamlined body; often characterized as a "turtle with a snake strung through it." Plesiosaurs were largely fish-eaters.
Pressure, selective	Changes in environmental conditions requiring corresponding changes in the form and function of a species as the alternative to extinction.
Prosauropoda	An infraorder of saurischian dinosaurs transitional between the early carnivores and the herbivorous Sauropoda.
Protoceratops	"Early horn-face," a primitive ceratopsian dinosaur.
Pseudosuchia	A thecodont suborder of archosaurs very likely ancestral to dinosaurs. Although they resemble crocodiles superficially (hence their name, "pseudo-crocodiles"), many pseudosuchians were well on the way to bipedal stature and endothermy.
Psittacosaurus	The "parrot-lizard," an ornithopod transitional to the ceratopsian dinosaurs.
Pterosaur	A "wing-lizard," one of the flying archosaurs whose wings were composed of leather airfoils supported on single elongated fingers.
Radiation, adaptive	A process in which the descendants of a successful organism diversify in form and function to occupy many econiches.
Reptilia	A class of terrestrial vertebrates including the lizards, snakes, turtles, and their extinct allies. Reptiles are ectotherms with three-chambered hearts; they were ancestral to both mammals and archosaurs.
Saltoposuchus	The "leaping crocodile," a bipedal thecodont archosaur.
Saltopus	"Leaping foot," a primitive coelurosaur. *Saltopus* was about the size of a house cat but lighter because of its hollow bones.
Saurischia	An order of dinosaurs whose hips superficially resemble those of lizards; hence the name "lizard-hips." The order includes both the carnivorous Theropoda and the herbivorous Sauropoda.

Sauropoda	The suborder of herbivorous dinosaurs with long necks and tails, believed to have been browsers on conifers and other tall trees. The Sinclair Oil Corporation Dinosaur is a typical sauropod. Sauropod means "lizard-foot," referring to the fact that these animals retain five toes, as do lizards. Sauropods normally walked on all fours, although some were apparently able to rise onto their hind legs to reach higher in the trees.
Saurornithoides	A Cretaceous coelurosaur with a large brain and forward-directed vision, whose name means "lizard like a bird."
Scelidosaurus	The "side lizard," a genus of primitive stegosaurs.
Specialization	The process in which an organism's form and function become more and more closely tailored to its econiche. A familiar example of specialization is the anteater of South America, which is very good at eating ants but can eat little else.
Stegosaur	Any of a family of dinosaurs armed with plates or spines along the spine—the name means "plated lizard."
Strata	Layers (singular, stratum) of rock or anything else. Rock strata contain a detailed record of the earth's history.
Struthiomimus	The "ostrich-mimic," a genus of advanced toothless coelurosaurs.
Styracosaurus	The "spiked lizard," a genus of ceratopsian dinosaurs equipped with long spikes mounted on the skull frill.
Symbiosis	"Living together," the condition of all living things on this planet. More specifically, an intimate association between two or more different kinds of organisms, as between herbivores and the plants on which they feed.
Syrmosaurus	The "dragging lizard," a primitive ankylosaur whose tail was originally believed to trail behind it on the ground.
Teratosaur	Any of a primitive family of carnosaurs of the Triassic, whose name means "monster lizard."
Thecodontia	The "socket-toothed" archosaurian order that gave rise to all later models such as crocodilians and birds.
Therapsida	An extinct order of vertebrates transitional between reptiles and mammals. The therapsids were endothermic but otherwise largely reptilian in structure.
Theropoda	The "beast-feet," a dinosaur suborder containing all of the carnivorous dinosaurs plus the prosauropods.
Torosaurus	"Bull-lizard," a genus of large Upper Cretaceous ceratopsian dinosaurs with gigantic heads and long facial horns.
Triceratops	"Three-horn-face," a genus of ceratopsian dinosaurs.
Tyrannosauridae	A family of Cretaceous carnosaurs, the largest and most specialized of carnivorous dinosaurs. The genus *Tyrannosaurus*, "tyrant-lizard," includes the largest known terrestrial predator.
Vertebrate	Any of a subphylum of Chordata possessing a bony or cartilaginous column of vertebrae protecting the main nerve cord.

BIBLIOGRAPHY

Those interested in pursuing further the evolution of the Archosauria will want to consult other books on the subject. Although much of the work that has been done on these animals remains hidden in technical journals deep within museum and university libraries, there are many popular works devoted to the subject. Best known perhaps are the several books by Edwin Colbert, possibly the greatest living exponent of vertebrate paleontology. Among these are *Dinosaurs: Their Discovery and Their World* (Hutchinson, 1962); *Men and Dinosaurs: The Search in Field and Laboratory* (Dutton, 1968); and *The Age of Reptiles* (Norton, 1966). The Finnish paleontologist Bjorn Kurten has compiled some interesting newer data on dinosaurs and the Mesozoic Era in his *The Age of the Dinosaurs* (McGraw-Hill, 1968). A classic and beautifully done (but probably partly erroneous) work on archosaur evolution may be had in the Dover Press edition of Gerhard Heilmann's *The Origin of Birds* (D. Appleton, 1972). In-depth discussion of dinosaur structure appears in the works of the late Alfred S. Romer, whose *Vertebrate Paleontology* (University of Chicago Press, 1966) and *The Vertebrate Body* (Saunders, 1949) or *The Shorter Version of the Vertebrate Body* (Saunders, 1971) are essential to the field. Finally, A. J. Desmond's *The Hot-Blooded Dinosaurs* (Dial, 1976) presents an interesting scholarly account of much of the furor presently surrounding the archosaurs' status among the vertebrates and, with a 1975 copyright, is one of the earliest books on this subject. Each of the above books offers a bibliography of its own, from which the interested reader may further broaden his understanding of the Archosauria.

INDEX